D0213004

Old Myths
and
New Realities
in
United States–Soviet
Relations

Old Myths and New Realities in United States–Soviet Relations

EDITED BY

Donald R. Kelley

AND

Hoyt Purvis

Foreword by J. William Fulbright

New York
Westport, Connecticut
London

Library of Congress Cataloging-in-Publication Data

Old myths and new realities in United States–Soviet relations / edited
  by Donald R. Kelley and Hoyt Purvis ; foreword by J. William
  Fulbright.
     p.   cm.
    Includes bibliographical references.
    ISBN 0–275–93498–5
    1. United States—Foreign relations—Soviet Union. 2. Soviet
Union—Foreign relations—United States. 3. United States—Foreign
relations—1989–   4. Soviet Union—Foreign relations—1985–
I. Kelley, Donald R. II. Purvis, Hoyt H.
E183.8.S65038   1990
327.73047—dc20   90–34368

Copyright © 1990 by Donald R. Kelley and Hoyt Purvis

All rights reserved. No portion of this book may be
reproduced, by any process or technique, without the
express written consent of the publisher.

Library of Congress Catalog Card Number: 90–34368
ISBN: 0–275–93498–5

First published in 1990

Praeger Publishers, One Madison Avenue, New York, NY 10010
An imprint of Greenwood Publishing Group, Inc.

Printed in the United States of America

∞

The paper used in this book complies with the
Permanent Paper Standard issued by the National
Information Standards Organization (Z39.48–1984).

10 9 8 7 6 5 4 3 2 1

Contents

Foreword

In 1964, while serving in the U.S. Senate, I made a speech that called attention to what I believed were some old myths and new realities having major significance for U.S. foreign policy and for international relations. At the time, I thought that there was an opportunity for a new approach to foreign policy, one that would abandon some of the old myths and move toward an improved relationship with the Soviet Union. Regrettably, although there were clear opportunities for improving relations, and even though the need for détente and arms control became steadily greater as both nations stockpiled nuclear weapons, it seemed that every opportunity for better relations was sidetracked.

Finally, with the coming to power of Mikhail Gorbachev in the Soviet Union and evidence of more serious interest on the part of the U.S. leadership in negotiating and cooperating with the Soviet Union, we have had the best chance since World War II to make a sensible adjustment in world affairs and to enable both nations to concentrate on their own serious domestic problems.

For decades we have been inclined to be suspicious of the Soviets and they of us, and I realize that there are those, including some contributors to this book, who remain suspicious and who are skeptical about real change occurring. However, I think that the evidence is clear and that we have a chance not only to improve governmental relations but to help break down some of the barriers of ignorance and misunderstanding that have contributed to the divisions among our nations. One important way to improve mutual understanding is through educational exchange. I would like to believe that one of the reasons for improved U.S.–Soviet relations has been the growing number of individuals who have had the opportunity to get to know the other country on a firsthand basis. I am encouraged by the fact that Politburo member Alexander Yakovlev, a key advisor to Gorbachev, was a Fulbright Scholar at Columbia University in 1958.

We have so much at stake in resolving our differences—for each of our nations and for international stability. I believe that there is an historic opportunity to bring an end to the old order in world affairs and for the great powers, the United States and the Soviet Union, to set an example for all nations. I strongly hope that we do not let this opportunity slip away.

—J. William Fulbright

Preface

This volume by a diverse group of experienced observers and analysts of U.S.–Soviet relations, Soviet affairs, and international relations is an outgrowth of a symposium organized by the Fulbright Institute of International Relations of the University of Arkansas.

The specific topic under consideration takes its cue from J. William Fulbright's 1964 book, *Old Myths and New Realities*, in which he called for a new approach to U.S. foreign policy, one that would abandon old myths and proceed on the basis of new realities, particularly in East–West relations. History will show that only limited progress was made toward meeting those goals in the short term. However, by the late 1980s it seemed appropriate to take a renewed look at myths and realities, especially in view of the significant changes that were occurring within the Soviet Union, in Europe, and in relations between the United States and the Soviet Union.

The contributors to this volume have observed U.S.–Soviet relations from a variety of perspectives—as academic specialists, diplomats, and journalists. They also represent a variety of viewpoints and opinions. We are grateful to them for sharing their insights and analyses on this subject, which will bear so significantly on the direction of world affairs in the 1990s.

We would also like to express our appreciation to others who contributed to the planning and/or the program of the Fulbright Institute symposium. These include colleagues from the Fulbright Institute and the University of Arkansas: Randall B. Woods, William E. Jackson, Jr., Peter Vanneman, David W. Edwards, Janet Tucker, Roy Reed, Marjorie Rudolph, Patricia O'Leary, David Gay, Thomas Kennedy, Ray Asfahl, William Bonner, Lisa Kelley, Mark Cory, and John Hehr. Others involved in the planning or program included Sergei Rogov, Vladimir Zhdanov, John Burrow, Graham Catlett, Welling Hall, Ronald W. Hart, Tom Henry, Gerald J. Janecek, Ross Marlay, Isabel S. Ryavec, Albert Zlabinger, and students Shannon Davis, Leighanne Hart, Dan Moore, Steve Powers, and Jeanne Witt.

We also express appreciation to the Arkansas Endowment for the Humanities for partial support of the program.

Special appreciation goes to Kim F. Wood and particularly to Betty Skinner for assistance in preparing the manuscript for this book.

1

U.S.–Soviet Relations and the Realities of Kremlin Politics

Donald R. Kelley and Hoyt Purvis

For four decades the Cold War and an adversarial relationship between the Soviet Union and the United States were seen as stark realities of international relations, dominating the world view of both nations, heavily influencing their domestic politics, and strongly affecting other nations around the world.

There were periodic thaws and episodes of détente, but by the early 1980s, they had given way to heightened hostility. The 1970s had been marked by a series of zigs and zags in relations, punctuated by arms-control agreements and summit meetings, and complicated by bouts of seemingly schizophrenic behavior on both sides with regard to the other. By the late 1970s the relationship was becoming increasingly troubled, as geostrategic concerns took on a sharper edge, and the 1979 Soviet invasion of Afghanistan cast a particularly long and ominous shadow.

When Ronald Reagan entered the White House in 1981 he made clear his hostility to the Soviet Union, which he later characterized as an "evil empire." He said that the only morality that Soviet leaders recognized was "what will further their cause, meaning they reserve unto themselves the right to commit any crime, to lie, to cheat in order to obtain that goal."[1]

It was a period marked by escalation in both rhetoric and arms buildups. The peak in the name-calling and perhaps the low point in the relationship occurred in 1983 after the Soviets shot down a Korean civilian aircraft. Reagan labeled the action a "crime against humanity." It later appeared that rather than deliberately shooting down a civilian airliner, the Soviets believed they were intercepting a military spy plane. The complete story may never be known. In any case, the atmosphere was harsh and bitter, reminiscent of the darkest days of the Cold War. Polemics were the order of the day.

Although the Soviets fired angry verbal blasts against the United States during much of this period, the Soviet international voice was actually somewhat muffled and relatively subdued, in part because it was a time of transition in Moscow. The increasingly stagnant Brezhnev regime came to an end in 1982, when the man who had been the Soviet leader for 18 years died. In his final years, Brezhnev had been in poor health and had played a limited public role. Brezhnev's successors, Yuri Andropov and Konstantin Chernenko, both died within a short time after taking office. It was an unsettled period in the Soviet Union, and neither Andropov (15 months) nor Chernenko (13 months) held power long enough to establish an international presence.

GORBACHEV AND CHANGE

Mikhail Gorbachev assumed power in Moscow in 1985. It was quickly apparent that Gorbachev, if for no reasons other than his health and relative youth (age 54), was a different type of Soviet leader. President Reagan said he was prepared to deal with Gorbachev with an open mind, but he doubted that Moscow's policies would change much. Oddly enough, it could be argued that the United States had grown rather complacent about the Soviet Union, at least in regard to the Soviet leadership and image in the world. The Soviets were seen as dangerous because of their military might and tendency to exploit volatile situations, especially in the Third World, but generally they were viewed as a rather plodding, if powerful, force in the world affairs. The Soviet economy was lagging seriously and Soviet diplomacy was notably undynamic. Many in the United States did not believe meaningful change in the Soviet

Union and in Soviet foreign policy was probable, regardless of the new leader; indeed, some doubted that it was possible.

Gorbachev had already caused a bit of a stir in the West when he visited Britain and was labeled by British Prime Minister Margaret Thatcher as the kind of leader with whom the West could "do business." The initial tendency, however, was to conclude that while Gorbachev represented a change in style, substance was another matter. His early international efforts were referred to, somewhat derisively, as a "charm offensive." His wit and his wife's stylish appearance turned heads but changed few minds in the West.

Meanwhile, Gorbachev plunged ahead vigorously, and when he began acknowledging Soviet problems and making changes to try to correct them, he began to be taken more seriously in the United States. Internationally, what had been seen as a "charm offensive" became a "diplomatic offensive" and a "peace offensive," and Gorbachev proved very adept in the international public relations competition. A tide of "Gorbymania" began to sweep across Europe, as many Europeans responded favorably to the Soviet leader's image and initiatives.

Increasingly, it became apparent that something different and important was underway, that Gorbachev had set in motion some of the most dramatic changes and developments in modern history, changes and events that in some respects went well beyond what he might have expected, and over which he couldn't always exercise much control. In any case, the changes Gorbachev initiated and unleashed were to recast global politics.

There are those in the United States and elsewhere, including some contributors to this volume, who remain highly skeptical about Gorbachev. However, even some of the skeptics acknowledge that Gorbachev moved far beyond what they had expected. Some make the point that Gorbachev was only doing what he had to do in order to try to rejuvenate and modernize his country. Indeed, Gorbachev, though a risk-taker, is a proven pragmatist, and he readily concedes that the Soviet Union needs more relaxed international conditions in order to concentrate attention and resources on its serious internal problems. In discussing his "new thinking," Gorbachev frequently emphasized the limitations he sees on the use of military power in today's interdependent world. Like the United States, the Soviets were discovering that military superpowers face constraints in what they can do abroad and have to consider the costs and consequences at home. Gorbachev recognized that Soviet involvement in Afghanistan was costly in a number of ways, and eventually he announced that he intended to withdraw Soviet forces. Some Western analysts said that Afghanistan would be a litmus test of Gorbachev's commitment to change. He announced a plan for withdrawal by 1989 and proceeded to live up to it.

REAGAN AND GORBACHEV

Some claim that the changes in Soviet policies under Gorbachev resulted from policies and actions of the Reagan administration—that the $2 trillion Reagan defense buildup, his proposed Strategic Defense Initiative (SDI), and the "Reagan Doctrine" of support for anti-Communist revolution or opposition (sometimes referred to by Reagan as support for "freedom fighters") in such areas as Afghanistan forced Gorbachev's hand. (Vladimir Pechatnov responds to this contention in Chapter Four of this book.) Whatever the impact of the Reagan policies on the Soviet leadership, there is strong reason to believe that domestic factors, not external ones, provided the primary motivation for Gorbachev.

Reagan and Gorbachev held their first summit meeting in Geneva in November 1985. Two years earlier Soviet negotiators had walked out of the Geneva arms talks in protest of the U.S./NATO decision to install Pershing II missiles in Western Europe and to continue developing SDI. Disputes over regional conflicts in the Third World and human rights issues in the Soviet Union also remained points of major controversy between the two countries. Reagan had previously shown little interest in a summit meeting, but his administration was under mounting pressure at home and abroad—partially because of the increasingly favorable international response to Gorbachev—to pursue arms-control negotiations more purposefully and to help reduce international tensions.

The Geneva summit did not achieve any breakthroughs in arms control, but there was an agreement to accelerate negotiations, and there was a sharp change in the international atmosphere. There was significant progress toward shattering some of the stereotyped views that had long haunted U.S.–Soviet relations. Reagan had done his part to perpetuate simplified notions about the Soviets, who in turn had often contributed their own regressive rhetoric.

STEREOTYPED MYTHOLOGY

The Soviet "threat" and anti-Communism had, of course, been major factors in U.S. politics for decades. Not only did U.S. foreign policy revolve around concerns about the Soviet Union and Communism, but at times those were also central considerations affecting domestic politics. American popular culture was permeated with Cold War spy thrillers and films in which Soviet characters and behavior were caricatured. In both the United States and the Soviet Union hostile and negative views of each other became ingrained. Exaggeration and oversimplification frequently characterized the way in which Soviets and Americans regarded or spoke of each other.

Andrei Mellville, a Soviet specialist on international relations, writes:

If the other state is seen as an "absolute enemy," as an "evil empire," as "the most inhuman system in human history," as an embodiment and receptacle of everything that is hateful, then the policy towards that state is based on these preconceptions, and in its turn leads to greater enmity.[2]

The same writer notes that such stereotypes and misconceptions hamper the search for mutually acceptable solutions and compromises. With the stakes so high in the nuclear age, such deep-rooted prejudices could undermine rational action. As Mellville says, "It is therefore particularly dangerous to dehumanize one's opponent, to turn the other side into an 'absolute evil' or an 'absolute enemy' devoid of any human traits." In his view, widespread anti-Soviet prejudice and biased information about the Soviet Union fixed in American minds the idea that it was a country "whose entire system of economy, politics, and ideology is completely hostile to the American one and poses a 'deadly challenge' to America."[3]

SUMMITS AND DIALOGUE

Steadily, Gorbachev was helping to change the atmosphere and to smash some of the old shibboleths about the Soviet Union. The

1985 Reagan–Gorbachev summit was an important step in this process. Gorbachev said then, "We agreed not to go on saying stupid things about each other."

As Georgi Arbatov, director of the Institute of U.S.A. and Canadian Studies in Moscow, suggested, Gorbachev was helping to deprive Americans of an enemy. At the same time, the Soviets were viewing the United States in much more placable terms.

The second Reagan–Gorbachev summit took place in Reykjavik, Iceland in 1986, primarily to continue the dialogue and to ratify the progress that had been made during the preceding year. Unexpectedly, the talks became much more wide ranging, however, and Gorbachev raised the possibility of a nuclear-free world by the year 2000, and Reagan suggested that both sides eliminate all ballistic missiles within ten years. Ultimately, the talks foundered over disagreement on SDI. Nonetheless, the groundwork had been laid for the INF (intermediate-range nuclear forces) treaty, which was signed when Gorbachev visited Washington in 1987. On his first visit to the United States, the Soviet leader scored another public relations triumph. Encouraged by the increasing openness within the Soviet Union, the advances in arms control, and the general improvement in U.S.–Soviet relations, Americans were receptive to the dynamic Gorbachev. At one point during his Washington visit, he halted his motorcade on a busy downtown street and plunged into the crowd, shaking hands like the most practiced U.S. politician.

THE NEW ERA

In 1988 another remarkable chapter in the new era of U.S.–Soviet relations occurred when President Reagan visited Moscow. In a particularly memorable vignette, with cameras trained upon them Reagan and Gorbachev strolled aimably through Red Square. In effect, Reagan pronounced the "evil empire" dead. Reagan said, "I was talking about another time, another era." Gorbachev, he said, was "different than previous Soviet leaders have been." For his part, Gorbachev said Reagan's remarks demonstrated "a sense of realism."

Considering conditions that had prevailed only a few years before, it did, indeed, seem like a new era in U.S.–Soviet relations.

It has been said of Gorbachev that he has accelerated history, and in many respects that is true. Certainly, he helped open the way for dramatic change—in the Soviet Union, Eastern Europe, and elsewhere. By 1989 Cold War barriers began to fall at a stunning pace, far more quickly than almost anyone imagined. Gorbachev became the symbol and embodiment of change and of hope for greater freedom, a catalyst for reform. Those challenging the status quo in Eastern Europe took some of their cues from Gorbachev, and when the Soviet leader refused to back the entrenched but highly unpopular governments in those countries, it was an undeniable signal for an end to the old regimes.

GLASNOST AND EXPECTATIONS

The countries of Eastern Europe could not have been kept walled off from what was occurring in the rest of the world any more than the Soviet Union could truly isolate itself from external influence or international trends. Once Gorbachev opened the door, *glasnost* proved to be a powerful force. But even before Gorbachev, the Soviet Union, despite its rigidity, was feeling and seeing the impact of the global telecommunications and transportation revolution and of external cultural influence. Citizens of the communist nations were increasingly aware of the economic vitality of the West, the freedom of movement, the dynamic nature of Western culture.

Gorbachev's lifting of many of the controls in the Soviet Union through his policy of *glasnost* heightened awareness of Soviet problems and shortcomings; it even opened the way for discussion of some of the worst aspects of Soviet history. And the *glasnost* of international communications helped carry Gorbachev's message and reshape the international image of the Soviet Union.

The dramatic changes that Gorbachev helped bring about have resulted in a more cooperative, if perhaps a more complicated, international atmosphere.

Dramatic as the changes have been in this new era, serious problems remain, and new ones have arisen within the Soviet Union and in its relations with the United States and the world. When the winds of change swept through the colonial world in the first decades after World War II, national leaders had to confront a tide of rising expectations among their peoples, expectations that were not always realistic or attainable. The winds of change that swept across the world in the late 1980s have created a new tide of rising expectations behind the old iron curtain. Fulfilling those expectations will be major challenge.

OLD REALITIES

While many observers, including the contributors to this volume, will argue over the degree to which Gorbachev has been the primary architect of the changing U.S.—Soviet relationship, few would challenge the notion that dramatic events in the Soviet Union and now in Eastern Europe have been and undoubtedly will continue to be central to defining this new reality. Few also would disagree that Gorbachev's "new thinking" and the policies it has produced find their motivation in the general secretary's oft-professed desire to deal with his nation's economic and social problems. While virtually all Soviet leaders since Stalin acknowledged that they lived in an exceptionally and possibly increasingly dangerous world, none has gone as far as Gorbachev in admitting that the Soviet version of Cold War conventional wisdom and the institutions that created and sustained it had become major roadblocks to both domestic and foreign policy reforms. As in the United States, the Kremlin had developed its own Cold War mentality, frightening in the sense that it held forth the specter of possible nuclear war but also reassuring in the sense that it gave clear mission and direction to national purpose and set understandable, if uncomfortable, limits on what the Soviet Union could hope to accomplish at home.

That raises two "old realities"—to play with the title of this book—that must be acknowledged if the complexity of these changes is to be understood. First, the relationship between any nation's domestic and foreign policies is exceptionally complex. It is never possible clearly to say that one "causes" the other. But it is possible to argue that choices in one area set parameters and limits, especially when resources are limited and leaders attempt to articulate policies that suggest that they are in control of events. In that sense, Gorbachev's domestic and foreign policy agendas are clearly linked both by his desire to forge a new view of his nation and its place in the world and by the economic, political, and social realities he finds at home.

The second old reality is that policies are never formulated in a vacuum. They find both inception and execution within the political realities confronting new leaders, and they are liberated to embody new ways of thinking or limited to a repetition of old shibboleths by that leader's ability to stretch and redefine those realities or by his failure to win control. While Soviet leaders know that in the long run they will be judged, at least in part, by their successes and failures in foreign policy, they also must be aware that in the short run they cannot hope to put their stamp on foreign policy until they have acquired control of the mechanisms of policy formation at home. Whatever his foreign policy objectives, no Soviet leader can hope to hold sway until he has taken control, however temporarily, of the levers of power and formulated a domestic agenda that gives direction and rationale to his policies abroad.

In noting and in many ways celebrating the widespread changes that have occurred in the Soviet Union and in Moscow's often troubled relationship with the outside world, we must also acknowledge that other old realities remain, at least as they pertain to the need for any new leader in the Kremlin to set forth an inspiring and effective agenda and to consolidate power within— or fundamentally change—the bureaucracies of party and government. No matter how much any new general secretary wishes to change the world around him, he is faced with realities and dilemmas that are of his predecessors' making. Some are institutional, rooted in ethos of single-party rule created by Lenin and given embodiment in the party-state machinery assembled by Stalin. Some are economic, or more correctly, allocational, confronting any Soviet leader with difficult trade-offs because of past commitments to conflicting military and civilian priorities and the deteriorating state of the economy. And some are a product of the two major conflicting tendencies of the post-Stalin era, one surviving from the Khrushchev era and offering the unsettling recognition that some kind of reform is necessary, and the second remaining as the legacy of the Brezhnev years and celebrating at least the appearance of success at home and abroad and the security of a "don't-rock-the-boat" conservatism.

As has every new Soviet leader before him, Gorbachev has attempted to shape his own version of the future starting with those realities and using the levers of power that were cobbled together by those who had risen to and held onto power before him. What follows in the succeeding chapters is an accounting of these attempts to bend old tools to frequently new tasks, especially in the critically important area of U.S.–Soviet relations. What has made Gorbachev unique, and what has accounted for his exceptional impact on the world around him, has been his willingness first to acknowledge the complexity and the interconnected nature of the problems confronting the Soviet Union and then to pursue sweeping broad-gauged remedies. Having grown to political maturity in the Brezhnev years, he had seen modest attempts at partial reforms fail, either because their vision was limited by ideological blinders or because the leadership lacked the political power or the will to force necessary changes. Even in his first years in power, Gorbachev was cautious in deed if not in word; while the brave new slogans of *perestroika* and *glasnost* came from the mouths and pens of the general secretary and his coterie, their actions seemed more reminiscent of the cautious reforms of the Andropov interregnum.

MOTIVATION AND INNOVATION

And then the Gorbachev we know today emerged—more willing to take risks both at home and abroad, more willing to encourage fundamental institutional change in at least some, if not all, of the heretofore sacrosanct features of the Leninist-Stalinist heritage, and more willing to acknowledge that the solution to any one problem required bold solutions to a host of other related difficulties.

Why the change, and is the Gorbachev strategy really that new? The first question is easier to answer, at least in terms of the motivations that led the general secretary to acknowledge that economic reforms required changes not only in the Stalinist economic mechanisms but also in the fundamental institutional structure, the nature of civil society, and the international role of his nation. The answer comes in two parts. The first lies in the objective reality that would have faced any general secretary attempting to deal with the problems that had accumulated during the Brezhnev years: tinkering and partial reforms would no longer work, either in the purely technical sense that they were inadequate to the task or in the psychological sense that they would have seemed little more than a timid more-of-the-same response by a new administration that had spoken boldly but failed to translate its words into deeds.

The second part of the answer lies in the political realities facing Gorbachev, who had risen over the years through a political system that bred caution, protected the institutional and personal prerogatives of the Soviet establishment, and prevented or nullified even modest reform efforts. If he had learned anything as the junior member of the Politburo under Brezhnev, it was that people and policies that rocked the boat soon were overcome by the direct opposition or the malevolent neglect of party and state bureaucracies. Any hope of reform had to cut through that Gordian knot of opposition, shaking up institutions that had been stable (and increasingly unresponsive) for 30 years since they had opposed Khrushchev's reforms, moving aside a whole generation of the nomenklatura whose tenacious grip on power had blocked change, and building new or reinterpreting old institutions and constituencies to respond to the programs and the personal leadership of the new general secretary.

How much of the Gorbachev phenomenon really is new? That depends on whether one intends the answer to deal with the policies of the new leadership or the mechanisms of making and implementing those policies—and no less with the question of how a new leader seizes control of the political agenda and consolidates his power. If the discussion deals with policy, the break with the past is striking: not only has Gorbachev launched new reforms virtually across the board, but also he has questioned (if not yet substantially changed) many fundamental features of the Stalinist institutional structure and the Leninist intellectual heritage. But if the question shifts to the levers of power—how a new leader formulates issues, seizes the agenda within the political and institutional parameters set for him both at home and abroad, manipulates people and institutions to consolidate power or to change those parameters, and struggles to reinterpret both his own and others' conventional wisdom when it blocks his efforts—then Gorbachev emerges in a more conventional light as a skilled player in the changing but always familiar game of Kremlin politics.

Without diminishing our appreciation of Gorbachev's bold innovations, we must still be reminded of the reality that he has faced the same tasks and found many of the same tactical, if not substantive, solutions employed by earlier Soviet leaders. So before we note what has changed, let us be reminded of what has remained constant.

DOMESTIC FACTORS AND WORLD ROLE

As has happened many times in the past, the domestic political agenda has shaped Moscow's foreign policy priorities. To be sure, domestic and foreign policy issues are symbiotically linked; economic and political choices at home occur within parameters set by the ability of Soviet leaders to manipulate the international milieu, symbolically or in reality, to create an external world seemingly receptive to their initiatives, just as foreign policy choices must take place within limits set by domestic realities. Most fundamentally, the Soviet interpretation of the hostile or friendly nature of the outside world has shifted widely in relation not only to the nature of such external realities but also in connection with Moscow's current economic priorities and with the waxing or waning fortunes of hardline or conciliatory factions within the Kremlin.

In historical perspective, any fundamental reorientation of political and economic priorities at home has always entailed a rethinking of Soviet attitudes on a number of foreign policy issues, including: the nature of the external world, especially the advanced capitalist nations; the definition of the Soviet Union's place in the international milieu as an outcast nation, a beleaguered champion of international socialism playing the game by its own rules, or a major superpower acting (more or less) by the rules of conventional diplomacy; Soviet goals in the international arena, including both short-term tactical considerations and long-term strategic options; the nature of legitimate national security needs, encompassing both an analysis of what constitutes adequate security and a discussion of the economic and social trade-offs at home; a reinterpretation of the nature and mechanisms of Soviet interaction with other nations, including conventional issues such as the use of bilateral and multilateral diplomacy, trade, and scientific and cultural exchanges, and less conventional mechanisms such as indigenous political movements and Communist parties, Soviet-influenced front organizations, and the like; the Soviet role in the Third World; and

Moscow's commitment to the international Communist movement. While different leaders have stressed varying elements of this panoply of responses and have offered different interpretations of external reality, each has dealt to some degree with the full range of issues.

No less is true of Gorbachev, whose "new thinking" addresses all of these questions, offering both a reinterpretation of the Soviet role in the world and a reassessment of the interplay of domestic and foreign policy priorities. The new leader's interest in shifting resources to solve long-standing economic problems at home and in increasing consumer production (undoubtedly to buy time for the other aspects of his reforms to succeed) requires that the world beyond Soviet borders be portrayed as less threatening and potentially more helpful and cooperative. Venturing farther than most of his predecessors, Gorbachev offers a vision of a new international reality focusing on the growing importance of commonly shared global problems and dealing with difficult political and economic issues with a growing sense of interdependence. Progress on conventional and strategic arms control and Moscow's tolerance of dramatic changes in Eastern Europe testify to its willingness to redefine the basic tenets of East-West relations and its own sense of national security, just as its diminishing commitment to regional conflicts and its arms-length attitude toward revolution in the Third World speak of its reduced attention to such peripheral issues.

Just as did his predecessors, Gorbachev also has sought to offer a dramatic program that both articulates his view of the future of the Soviet Union and its international role and rationalizes his own consolidation of power. To be sure, past general secretaries have differed strikingly in terms of the scope and ambition of their programs. Stalin's doctrine of "Socialism in One Country" envisioned the transformation of the Soviet Union into an industrial state, Khrushchev's new party program called for the Soviet Union to enter into the beginning stages of communism by the 1980s, and Brezhnev's notion of developed socialism forecast the beginnings of post-industrial society in the Soviet Union even as it rationalized the growing stagnation of the society. The question of their success aside, each program was a political formula, a combination of pie-in-the-sky futurology (albeit rationalized in the then-current reinterpretation of Marxism–Leninism), a short-term political agenda, and—perhaps most important—a set of ideas, slogans, and marching orders that defined the issues the way the new general secretary wanted them defined and focused activity on the attainment of his political goals.

Gorbachev has been no less bold in offering his own program—and so successful in selling the ideas (if not the accomplishments) contained within it that the slogans of *perestroika, glasnost,* and *demokratizatsiia* have entered into our own vocabulary. While the details of that program and its implications for U.S.–Soviet relations occupy the chapters that follow, it is appropriate at this point to ask a more basic question: do Gorbachev's program and the political, social, and economic changes that have been undertaken in its name constitute a fundamental reorientation of Soviet thinking about the nature of their society and its world role—what a Marxist would term a shift from quantitative to qualitative change—or are they merely at best adjustments of convenience tinkered together for political expediency or at worst attempts to deceive both domestic and foreign audiences? Needless to say, opinions will vary, as they do among our contributors.

CRITERIA FOR REFORM

While these introductory comments cannot hope to anticipate the answers, they will suggest four criteria by which the reform efforts may be judged. First, the comprehensive nature of reforms must be weighed against the past experience of unsuccessful piecemeal efforts; the more extensive and wide-ranging the reform agenda, the more likely that a serious attempt is being made to deal with inseparably related problems. By this criterion, Gorbachev's efforts receive high marks, at least in terms of the rhetoric of reforms. Second, the institutionalization of reform efforts measures both the regime's intent to translate promises into action and the attempt to dislodge real or potential opposition. Here, too, Gorbachev has moved farther than his predecessors, with the exception of Stalin's institutionalization of a single-party system bent on rapid industrialization, especially in terms of shifting power from the party to the government and creating a legal basis for a cautious form of Soviet democracy. Third, new political agendas that have coincided with widespread personnel changes throughout the nomenklatura or in the rise of a whole new generation of Soviet leaders have been more likely to take strong hold and leave their imprint on history.

The passage of Stalin's class of 1939—the generation that rose to power after the purges and remained in office until the mid-1980s—may now be followed by Gorbachev's self-described "children of the 20th Party Congress," who will complete the reform agenda begun three decades ago by Khrushchev. And finally (fourth) and less tangibly, the leader's own dedication to reform and his political skill and courage are important factors in his and his program's survival. On this point Gorbachev also receives high marks for his own tenacity in pursuing his programs, for his political skill in turning adversity to tactical advantage (witness his handling of Chernobyl and the Mathias Rust incidents), and for positioning himself as the only reasonable middle-of-the-road figure within an increasingly divided leadership.

RESHAPING THE NATION

As has every new general secretary before him, Gorbachev also has had to deal with the problem of consolidating power. In conventional wisdom, this has usually meant capturing control of the party apparatus from the grassroots upward, using the nomenklatura to pack successively higher party bodies with supporters. But in Gorbachev's case, the process has been reversed; the new general secretary moved first against his opponents in the Politburo and Secretariat and only later forced his critics in the Central Committee from office.

The shift of real power from the party's policy-making bodies and the apparatus to the new legislature, Council of Ministers, and the new presidency is another innovative if not totally unprecedented maneuver; just as Stalin made use of the newly created office of general secretary to consolidate his power and Khrushchev revitalized a moribund party and gave it a central role vis-à-vis the government, Gorbachev has redefined the role of key institutions to throw his opponents off balance. No less important is the identification of a new constituency in whose name the new leader launches reforms. Just as Stalin spoke for the class of 1939, Khrushchev for a party machinery that had been pushed again, and Brezhnev for a generation of entrenched bureaucrats, so Gorbachev speaks for a new generation of reformers within the intelligentsia and to a broader public audience mobilized and given voice through his democratic reforms.

Certainly there are dangers in Gorbachev's approach. Building new institutions is a risky business, especially when the old ones cling to the last vestiges of power and influence. And any attempt to mobilize a broader public constituency and to create what Gorbachev has termed a Soviet "civic culture" respectful of democratic institutions runs the risk of setting loose a revolution of rising expectations and demands. No less significant is the questionable fate of economic reforms. Politics aside, there is a good case to be made that the average Soviet citizen—and perhaps one should exclude the border republics, where nationalism is the motivating force—will judge Gorbachev and his *perestroika* less in terms of the procedures of democratic rule, or the number of arms-control agreements signed, and more in terms of his or her standard of living. And the real paradox is that Gorbachev will have given to that citizen a mechanism—the new Congress of People's Deputies and the Supreme Soviet—through which his or her voice may now be heard.

Only one other Soviet leader since the revolution has reshaped his nation so boldly: Joseph Stalin. The comparison is important not because of the suggestion that, the late Andrei Sakharov to the contrary, Gorbachev will emerge as a new supreme leader, a vozhd in his own right. Nothing in Gorbachev's program, and more important in the established pluralism of Soviet society, suggests that this will occur. But the comparison is appropriate in another sense: not since the early years of Stalin's rule has the Soviet Union been at such a potential turning point when ideologies, institutions, and world views were open to redefinition. The hopeful feature of this reality is that all questions are now open, and the range of possibilities dazzles even the most skillful Kremlin watcher; but the frightening feature is that the answers to these questions will shape the Soviet Union and its relations with the world well beyond the political careers and lives of today's players, just as the Stalinist system and the Cold War shaped the last half century. Whatever emerges will set the mold not only for the new generation of leaders now coming to power in Moscow but also for those of us in the West and elsewhere who must deal with the Soviet Union well into the next century.

NOTES

1. Ronald Reagan, White House Press Conference, January 29, 1981.

2. Andrei Mellville, *How We View Each Other: The Enemy Image and New Political Thinking* (Moscow: Novosti Press Agency Publishing House, 1988), p. 5.

3. Ibid., p. 21.

2

Perestroika and Soviet Relations with the West

Jerry F. Hough

It is going to take us some time to really comprehend *perestroika*. What is occurring now is a very fundamental debate over the precise meaning of socialism. We have taken for granted that what the Soviet Union has is socialism—that big ministries, planning from the center, and a one-party system is what socialism means. Now there are people like Mikhail Gorbachev who say that was actually deformed socialism.

Beyond this debate on the definition of socialism, the real questions that interest us have to do with its implications for Moscow's relationship with the West. After all, if a market economy is introduced in the Soviet Union and the Soviets become more hostile to us, does it really matter in terms of U.S.–Soviet relations if they introduce the market? But if, on the other hand, the reform goes relatively slowly but the Soviets totally change their foreign policy, the improvement in bilateral ties would be a major plus. What we really ought to examine is not simply the details of how various domestic reforms work, but the question of whether the Soviet Union is changing its basic relationship to the West. To what extent is this change real? Are we seeing something that is going to be minor, or are we seeing major change? Are we seeing something that is truly a watershed in history?

My opinion is that we are at a watershed, that in many ways what is occurring—although the Soviets will never admit it—is a repudiation of some of the essence of the 1917 revolution. Mikhail Gorbachev says he is going back to Lenin. But in many ways the Soviets are repudiating at least 50 percent of the essence of Lenin. I believe that in foreign policy terms, the 1917 revolution was a rejection of the West, a rejection of Western civilization, as the U.S. conservatives rightly used to say. I think the Soviets are now essentially reintegrating their nation back into the West. That reintegration is very important, for it is altering the structure of international relations. Much that we have taken for granted is in the process of change.

ASSUMPTIONS AND ANCIENT TRUTHS

My belief is that in ways we really have not yet understood, we have changed many of our assumptions about the Soviet Union. If we remember the assumptions that we had in the 1940s and 1950s, and we understood them and thought them through, we would know much better why Gorbachev is to be taken seriously than if we follow the fads of interpretation that are coming out of Moscow's intelligentsia. Remembering some of the old ancient truths is, I believe, a better guide to understanding what is going on than is listening to the cliches that we hear now. The cliches say that the bureaucrats rule in the Soviet Union and that they are conservative, that Gorbachev is too weak to institute change, and that he is willing to let the country muddle on. But all of these cliches, which are often heard from Moscow's intelligentsia, are totally contradictory to things that we believed 20 or 30 years ago. In my opinion, what we believed then is much closer to the truth.

Consider the question of bureaucratic and worker resistance to Gorbachev's reforms. It used to be said that as the number of people in the educated middle class increased, so would the pressure for democratization. But now there is an inclination to say, "No, no, Gorbachev wants change, but the Soviet people don't want it. They want to cling to their old repression." We no longer talk about the Soviet middle class as a positive force for change. We talk about conservative bureaucrats, and that seems to me to be utter nonsense. We forget that the bureaucracy itself was repressed. We should remember that in many ways, even today, this is a dictatorship.

It is nonsense to say that there is a privileged bureaucracy in the Soviet Union, except for perhaps the top 50 or 100 people. In many ways, the bureaucrats have been as much the victims as the villains. The bureaucratic class itself is incredibly underprivileged. The bureaucrats are better off than collective farmers, but they do not have anywhere near the kind of good life that bureaucrats have in Madrid, London, or Vienna. They haven't had free newspapers to read, good films and television to watch, or freedom to travel. They haven't had the security of private property. The notion that these people who are at the top—whose income is far less than the income of the middle class in the West and who are far less free than the middle class in the West—want to cling to the old repression is blind to the reality of the past repression of the bureaucrats themselves.

In 1964, there were 30 million people with a high school diploma or better in the Soviet Union. Now there are 125 million, more than four times as many. These are people who in a socialist system go to work for the bureaucracy. They are the bureaucrats, the professionals, and the managers, and I think they want more freedom and constitute the bulk of Soviet public opinion that advocates reform.

CONSOLIDATING POWER

We also sometimes hear that Gorbachev cannot assert leadership vis-à-vis the Politburo, the Central Committee, or individual opponents such as Igor Ligachev. That is not what we said about the power of a general secretary in the 1940s and the 1950s. Then we said that this is a system in which the dictator is able to consolidate power within the party. He appoints the regional party bosses, these bosses control the delegates to the party congresses, and the party congresses control the Central Committee and the Politburo. But now somehow Gorbachev is supposed to be weak vis-à-vis other members of the Politburo. However, by all of the traditional standards, this has been the most rapid consolidation of power in Soviet history. Remember that from March 1953 to March 1957, the four years when Khrushchev was consolidating power, he was able to remove one man from the Politburo. In Brezhnev's first four years, he removed two aging members from that body. In Gorbachev's first four years, he removed seven out of nine Politburo members. He replaced them with essentially non-entities. Moreover, Gorbachev has managed to position himself comfortably in the middle, between the right and the left, leaving him free to play one off against the other.

Gorbachev has been sensitive to the potential power of the Central Committee to remove him. Not only did he postpone radical policy change until after the 27th Party Congress in 1986 replaced the Central Committee elected in 1981, but also he even persuaded one-quarter of the voting members of the 1986 Central Committee to resign "voluntarily" three years later. By making himself chairman of the Supreme Soviet (that is, president), removable only in open session by a Congress of People's Deputies that is more reform-minded than the Central Committee, he has made it virtually impossible for the Central Committee to remove him without a test of strength in the streets. If he is overthrown as general secretary, the only way he can also be removed as chairman of the Supreme Soviet is to have an extraordinary open session of the congress. In the interim he has one whole week to organize people and to get them out into the streets.

The fact that he is now elected by the congress does not make him democratic; on the contrary, it makes him a kind of dictator much more difficult for the inner circle to overthrow. Although major liberalization is occurring, it is not democratization in the sense that Gorbachev can be removed from power by some kind of free election. He is able to use the situation, essentially, to strengthen his position. But if we go back to the old wisdom about Soviet policies and are careful not to confuse it with the U.S. expectation that conflict between the "branches"—in the Soviet case, the new legislature and the party—is inevitable and likely to persist, we see again that the Soviets have a system that is constructed to facilitate the consolidation of power by the general secretary. Gorbachev has used it like a master.

There is another frequently heard objection. It is conceded that Gorbachev is strong and that there is basic support for what he is doing. But why, it is asked, would he let foreign ideas penetrate to his people? And why would he basically reduce the powers of his office or the power of the ministries? Why would he let the Estonians have a little bit more freedom? Why would be loosen control over Eastern Europe?

I think, again, that parts of the ancient wisdom are right. We used to say that the leader is interested both in personal power and in national power, and I think that is true. But, paradoxically, it is precisely because Gorbachev is interested in personal and national power that he is giving up the kind of power we thought he had, but which in reality was illusory. The fact is, when the ministries in Moscow control the stores and the hospitals and the factories, that does not mean Gorbachev controls them. In a sense, Alan Greenspan, who can raise interest rates, can have a larger and more immediate impact on the U.S. economy than a general secretary can have on the Soviet economy. Gorbachev wants to use levers that are more efficient. He does not care whether the hospital in Baku operates by directive from the Ministry of Health in Moscow or whether it operates under local control; he simply wants good results. The mechanisms of the old system didn't give him those results, so he increases power to do what he wants by using a different mechanism. Ends rather than means become the central criterion of judgment.

If we go back to the general questions—Why is Gorbachev opening up to Western ideas, Why would he cut the military, Why does he seem to be giving up some kind of power?—I think that there is another piece of ancient wisdom that we should recall. It is a piece of ancient wisdom that we still believe when we talk about the United States, but not when we talk about the Soviet Union: protectionism is bad for economic growth. This is an absolute fundamental of U.S. economics, one place where the right and the left agree. Economists at both ends of the spectrum agree that protectionism and interference with the market are bad for economic efficiency. I agree with that wisdom. However, we never apply it to the Soviet Union. The fact of the matter, though, is that the Soviet Union has total protectionism.

TWO IRON CURTAINS

The essence of the Soviet system has been two iron curtains: one against modern Western ideas, and the other against Western market forces. Even when the Soviets imported goods and technology, the crucial thing was that Soviet manufacturers never lost any business. That is what protectionism means. In the Soviet system, even when you import foreign technology, local manufacturers are not compelled to compete against it. Thus, the Soviet Union has created a kind of total protectionism that is more effective than tariffs. Also, the Soviets have not had to export manufactured goods and compete in the world market. If Soviet manufacturers were forced to export, they would encounter competition in the foreign market and be forced to raise the quality of their products. Yet Soviet manufacturers have been under no pressure to export. So they had to compete neither with any foreign imported goods nor in foreign markets.

For 60 years there has been a monopolistic Ministry of Automobiles, Ministry of Tractors, Ministry of Electronics, and so on, totally protected from foreign competition. The results reflect exactly what an economics textbook would predict: total protectionism means total economic disaster in terms of quality, competitiveness, responsiveness, and efficiency. The result has been that the Soviet Union lags even behind a country like South Korea. The Soviet Union started industrializing at the same time as Japan, and both were destroyed in World War II. But Japan is in another league now. Protectionism, or at least the Soviet version, has brought not an increase in national power, but rather a reduction of national power.

NATIONAL POWER

If you are a Soviet leader concerned with this reduction of national power, you have got to attack protectionism in order to defend yourself against the growing economic power not only of the European countries, China, and Japan, but also of a number of emerging nations that now are internationally competitive economically and soon will be world or regional powers in every sense of the term. How can a Soviet leader not want to bring his nation up to competitive world standards if he is interested simply in preserving national power? And if national power demands an end to protectionism, it demands travel abroad to open up the nation to outside influences so that foreign markets can be understood. Until the Soviets travel and learn the foreign market, until they read foreign newspapers, until they understand foreign advertising, they will never be in the top ranks of the world economy. Until they have their own multinationals, until they have the kind of integration into the world economy that the United States and Japan now possess, they will not be fully competitive, and in the future, such competitiveness is the key to national power.

If we believe that the Soviets want national power vis-à-vis that changing outside world, and if we believe that total protectionism means economic disaster, which of our ancient wisdoms do we want to surrender? Do we want to believe that the Soviets are not interested in power anymore? Do we want to give up the ancient wisdom that you can have economic growth and power without economic competition?

The notion that the Soviets are going to stagnate economically is just wishful thinking on the part of some. Look at the situation: the preservation of national power demands reform, and Gorbachev has an educated middle class that wants more freedom and the security of the market. To think that these factors will not work in the direction of freedom denies everything that we know about the world. When populations are uneducated and poor, it is very difficult to create a democracy. But when countries become middle class and educated, dictatorships vanish from the scene. It was true in Western Europe, then in Southern Europe, in Spain and Portugal, in Greece, in Brazil, in Argentina, in South Korea, and now in Eastern Europe. To think that the Soviets are going to be different, that they do not want freedom, or that they are willing to be a Third World country, goes against everything that we know. There will be ups and downs, and there will be problems. But we would have to give up some extremely basic beliefs if we do not think the drive for opening the Soviet Union to the West and integrating it into the world economy is very strong.

FOREIGN POLICY IMPLICATIONS

If I am even 50 percent correct, the foreign policy implications are enormous. We have argued over whether Soviet foreign policy is expansionist, defensive, or opportunistic. Somehow that misses the point. It is both expansionist and defensive. Soviet behavior has been unacceptable in some cases, but the policy of most great powers, often including the United States, has been unacceptable to some. Has Soviet policy been that different from other great powers? Unfortunately, it has not.

But something else has been enormously peculiar about Soviet foreign policy. Its essence is not caught in phrases like expansionist or defensive. For me, the central essence of Soviet foreign policy is not reflected in what it has done in Afghanistan, in arms control, or in Nicaragua. It is reflected in the fact that in 1982—and it is basically true today—the capital of the Soviet Union did not have a single French restaurant or a single Italian restaurant. You can understand that they might not like the ideas of Solzhenitsyn or that they might not like capitalist propaganda. But what have they got against French food, or Mexican food, or Japanese food? And is it not strange that they do not ever hire any foreigners? After all, Hollywood hires foreign actors, the opera in Milan hires foreign singers, but the Bolshoi Ballet would never hire a foreigner. What is political about the ballet? Why was there an iron curtain against the abstract art of Picasso, who was a Communist and whose work was basically left wing?

There is a strangeness about the Soviet Union, not simply in policy terms, but in its relationship to the outside world, that I think is well caught in the theory of totalitarianism. That theory says left-wing extremism and right-wing extremism are the same, whether they are called Stalinism or Nazism. If you apply this to the right-wing extremism we know today, such as that associated with Khomeini, and you say left-wing extremism and right-wing extremism are similar, that is another way of saying that Lenin was the Khomeini of Soviet history, and that the Bolshevik revolution was the Khomeini revolution of its day. I think this conclusion is basically true. That is, I think that just as Khomeini revolted against modern Western culture, which he considered satanic, the essence of the Communist revolution was not against capitalism, but against what the Marxists call the superstructure of capitalism—the ideas, the culture, the politics, and the values of Western civilization, which Marx said has no inherent value other than to serve the interests of the dominant class.

The Bolshevik revolution was really the rejection of modern Western civilization. This explains the curious Soviet notion that there is something evil about modern art or French restaurants. It is not rational, but that, I think, is the essence of what Communism has been. And it also has been the essence of the Soviet relationship with the outside world. What we have to understand is that when Gorbachev speaks of a common European home, he is talking about reintegrating his nation into the achievements of Western civilization.

In broader historical terms, the old attitude toward the modern West is disappearing. Essentially, the kids who wanted blue jeans and jazz and who were in their twenties in the 1950s are now the members of the Politburo and the Central Committee. Perhaps they don't want blue jeans anymore, but they do want to be part of Western civilization.

THE COMMON EUROPEAN HOME

Putting this in broader historical terms, that is, looking away from the purely Soviet aspects, what is going on has to be understood as being the great historical event of the last 40 years. If you ask what was the great achievement of the postwar period, it was not, as some have said, that the Cold War was successful or that we contained the Soviet Union. That was an achievement, but the greater achievement is that we ended 400 years of war among the Western Europeans. In 1939 who would have thought that war would become so unthinkable between England, France, and Germany or between the United States and Japan? The great achievement is essentially that we have created a common Western European home of 600 million people, from the Elbe River in West Germany to San Francisco across the Atlantic.

If you ask what is happening now and what is going to happen over the next 20 or 30 years, it is that the Soviets now are joining our European home. I believe that in 20 years war between the Soviets and the other Europeans will be as unthinkable as war is today between the English and Germans. That is hard to imagine, but in 1939 it would have been hard to imagine the world of today. We are moving toward a world in which there will be a common European home from Vladivostok to San Francisco.

There are several reasons for the emergence of a common European home that includes the Soviets. One is simply that the Soviets want it. They are Europeans. Pushkin and Tolstoy were Europeans, and those were the writers Gorbachev memorized when he was in school. They expressed the values of the Westernized elite of Peter the Great that the revolution overthrew, and those values are still there. The Soviets want to be part of Europe because they feel that they are European, that they come out of an orthodox version of a common Christian civilization.

I believe the Soviet Union is joining this common European home partly for reasons of defense. By the year 2150, India and China will have become superpowers. There are going to be a billion Indians, more than a billion Chinese, and I think the Soviets have a sense that if they remain a semibackward country, they are not going to be major actors on the world stage. They have the sense that they want to be part of a billion Europeans playing in the league of the new superpowers, joined together with the Europeans and the Americans for defense purposes vis-à-vis the non-Western world.

MEANING FOR THE UNITED STATES AND THE WORLD

In conclusion, what is to be said about the relationship of all this to the United States? In longer terms, if my image is essentially accurate, or even 50 percent accurate, I think the Gorbachev revolution is a good thing for the United States. We have experienced much paranoia about the Soviets, and if this begins to fade it has to be beneficial for the U.S. political system. I think to be perfectly frank, that our grandchildren and our great-grandchildren are going to be glad to be on the side of a billion Europeans.

The Gorbachev revolution is good for the United States in the short run, too, if we would like to take advantage of it. We like to think of the 1980s as a period in which we stood tall, in which U.S. power increased. That is not the way history is going to look at it. Our relationship with the Soviet Union looked very good in the 1980s, but the Soviet Union was not our real adversary. We had already basically defeated the Soviet Union by 1980. Our challenges in the 1980s came from Japan and from the emerging European Community. Our power vis-à-vis like Japan is much weaker now that it was in 1980, and every year that we continue to go more than $100 billion in debt to foreigners, our national power is further eroded. To the extent that Gorbachev's economic problems give us the chance to reduce an unnecessary military presence in Europe under conditions that still guarantee security and allow us to reduce our deficit and become more economically competitive, that is good for our national power in the short run.

There are, of course, problems in the short run. As I have pointed out, the great achievement of the post-war period was the end of conflict among England, France, and Germany, and between Japan and the United States—and the Soviet threat played a very useful role in that. Sometimes we exaggerated the Soviet threat precisely to end the kind of conflicts that had devastated the world twice in this century. But now if the Soviet threat disappears—and it clearly is disappearing, or at least the perception of a threat is disappearing—we and the Japanese, we and the Europeans, the Europeans and the Japanese, are left with our economic tensions now at center stage.

We are in a situation in which the question of the reunification of Germany is on the agenda again, in which the whole question of the Japanese-Soviet relationship is on the table. The problem of how to maintain Western unity at a time when we must reduce our deficit and deal with the reunification of Germany will put a strain on the Western alliance. These are not trivial questions, and we will not have the Soviet threat to serve as the glue to hold us together. We are in a difficult transitional period that I hope we can get through without major problems. But what is absolutely crucial is to recognize that we have more than one problem. We cannot simply say that we are not absolutely certain whether Gorbachev will be successful. I think the odds are 90 to 95 percent that that process is going forward, but there is a chance that it will fail. What is clear is that problems are coming in the Western alliance, in the Atlantic community, and in the Japanese-U.S. relationship. If we try to maintain the sense of a Soviet threat, if we bury our heads in the sand in a way that lets events get out of control, the danger is that it will smash the achievements of the post-war world, achievements that have prevented a great depression and that have unified the West.

The world is not changing overnight. This is a process that will take 5, 10, 15, or 20 years. But if the United States has the illusion that the old world is going to last forever, that we do not have to think about Gorbachev or that we can wish him away, we will continue to experience the decline of power that we have seen in recent years—likely accompanied by crises in our alliances, which may cost us very dearly.

3

The Changing Relationship: An American View

William G. Miller

We in the United States have had to contend with the Soviet Union as a major fact of life for many years, and that contention has shaped the nature of our lives. We have had to go to war because of the activities of the Soviet Union. We fought on the same side in World War II, although most of the time we thought of ourselves as enemies. Despite our mutual preoccupation, however, we know very little about each other. It has been very difficult in most cases to really see each other firsthand. We have had, in the past, to accept what we know about each other from the most indirect means. Even the U.S. government, with all of its resources—what our diplomats were able to glean, what journalists were able to fathom, what defectors were able to tell us, what emigres were able to inform us, what spies were able to steal—produced a very incomplete picture. And it is only now, within the last few years, that as ordinary citizens we have the capacity and the possibility of getting on an airplane and seeing for ourselves what the reality is. And more and more of us on both sides are doing that. We can now witness the change taking place, and we are changing as a result, partially as a consequence of this increased contact.

I have had to live all of my life with the problem of what to do about the Soviet Union. I was born and brought up in New York in the 1930s. New York, being the cosmopolitan city that it is, had many immigrants from all over the world and, of course, emigres from the Soviet Union. The view of the Soviet Union that I grew up with, largely shaped by the experience of these recent Soviet immigrants, was that it was a dangerous place, that it was a dictatorship, that it was cruel to its people, that there was tremendous waste of men and resources, and that it was a great stain on humanity. And these opinions of recent immigrants were certainly reinforced by reality. The experience under Joseph Stalin, which we heard about from victims of that experience who came to the United States, only deepened the atmosphere of suspicion about the Soviet Union in which I grew up.

We had good reasons to believe that the Soviet Union was an enemy to the United States. We tended to forget, however, that in World War II we were allies against a common enemy: the brutal tyranny, the fascism, the horror of Nazi Germany and its allies. In that common purpose of defeating Hitler we were able to join together to defeat something that, no matter how much we distrusted one another, was found to be more reprehensible. At the same time, overshadowing the courage and sacrifice of the Soviet Union, our comrade-in-arms in Great War against Nazi Germany, was the fact that it was ruled by one of the most heinous leaders of all time, Joseph Stalin.

In 1953, the year I graduated from Williams College, Stalin died. This event should have been a great turning point in history, but old myths persist, and the notion that something else—a government with decent purposes—might be possible in the Soviet Union, died hard. Even with the coming of a radically different kind of leader in the form of Nikita Khrushchev, we continued to look at the Soviet Union as an enemy, as an abuser of human rights, as a place of tyranny, where the human spirit meant little and where power for a few meant much. I can remember the courses that I took on Soviet history, and on Russian history and literature. The books that we used as texts and the teachers who taught me and the articles that were written in the journals and newspapers all reinforced the dark perceptions about the Soviet Union that I had as I was growing up. That was a perception, an experience shared by many in this country.

Reading tea leaves—Kremlinology—was the way that we saw evidence of distinctions in the Soviet Union. But underneath that difficult process of careful reading of texts and official statements, observing the positioning of leaders on platforms at May Day parades, studying defector reports and emigre interviews, and odds and ends of insight that might creep into the meager data banks, the basic premise, the old myth that persisted, was that the Soviet Union equalled Stalin. This fundamental view was only reinforced when the United States became enmeshed in the Vietnam War and the struggle elsewhere for influence in the Third World, where our competition with the Soviets took the form of military action—in almost all cases by proxy, or in the back alleys of the world, as Dean Rusk used to describe intelligence warfare.

We were at war, even if it was a cold war fought in remote regions of the world. It was a war that was defined by official policy. The most important policy statement of the early Cold War period, the 1950 National Security Council paper that became known as NSC–68, fully described in rich, bellicose rhetoric the Soviet Union as our most formidable enemy.[1] The prevailing view was that we had no choice but to arm in order to contain a great superpower that, if left uncontained, would move with great military power to destroy us. Containment of a powerful, hostile enemy was our policy, our belief, our understanding.

When did the change in our beliefs and perceptions begin to occur? Certainly, within the Soviet Union itself there had always been resistance to the pattern that Stalin had established. However, it was really only when the Soviet Union itself began to examine in public what it had done in its 70 years that change began. In the early 1980s, after the death of Leonid Brezhnev and what the Soviets call the "period of stagnation," stock began to be taken of the Soviet past. They looked at their society politically, economically, culturally, socially—in every possible way. Very interestingly, they looked at the state of their society, most deeply in very remote places like the Academy of Sciences in Novosibirsk. Work was also being done in the academies of science in Moscow and Leningrad. Maverick intellectuals like Roy Medvedev, the great historian, and extraordinary scientists like the hydrogen-bomb maker Andrei D. Sakharov, the Nobel Peace Prize human-rights activist, also began to look at the nature of their society and its place in the world. What they found was that the Soviet Union's political system had failed, the economic system was in serious jeopardy, and the official culture bore little relationship to the realities of social life, needs, or desires in the Soviet Union.

At the same time, there was a recognition that events in the world, the danger of nuclear annihilation, the possible destruction of the planet's environment, and the problems of poverty, disease, and underdevelopment were such scourges that they could be dealt with not by any single nation, no matter how powerful, but could only be solved by cooperative measures of all nations. It was this recognition that brought about the beginnings of the transformation that we are now witnessing in the United States in attitudes toward the Soviet Union and the transformation in public attitudes in the Soviet Union itself. This recognition—that there had to be cooperative measures rather than competition in order to survive—is the most meaningful change and is the basis of what the Soviets under Gorbachev call the "new thinking." It is a notion that many of us in the United States have come to accept as valid for own reasons, but we have done so on the basis of our own evidence. It is this common recognition that we must cooperate if we are to survive that has brought about the possibility for doing away with old myths and has given us the means to face those very present new realities.

On the political, economic, and cultural fronts the changes in Moscow come largely from internal causes in the Soviet Union. We in the United States have had very little to do with those changes, although the consequences of those changes affect us greatly. The new notions of liberty; the more open attitude toward human rights, political freedom, what an economy is for, what one does with one's power; there are all questions that are openly discussed within the Soviet Union and with us. It seems to me that we are now in a position, after 70 years of uncertainty, of coming to a more hopeful relationship than we ever have. It seems to me that for the first time there is hope that we can live in stable, sensible, long-term peaceful ways without the fear of war.

CHANGES IN U.S. PERCEPTIONS AND ATTITUDES

Every serious poll that I know of that has been taken in the last few years on the subject of the U.S.–Soviet relations shows with convincing evidence that there have been profound changes in U.S. perceptions of the Soviet Union. The polls also show profound changes in U.S. attitudes about what the relationship between the two great superpowers should be. Some important and extraordinarily thorough polling on U.S.–Soviet relations has been undertaken, particularly in the project called "Americans Talk Security." In this project, three different polling organizations worked together on developing a very detailed, extremely sophisticated analysis of U.S. thinking about the Soviet Union, Gorbachev, and what our policies should be. Twelve polls were taken over a period of two years, and they showed an overwhelming majority, in the 80 percent range, that is aware that a great change is taking place and that is hopeful it could be for the best. So there is optimism and there is awareness of a possibility of better relations. This is a great change in U.S. attitudes. Second, a great personal popularity has surrounded Mikhail Gorbachev, equal to that, remarkably, of Ronald Reagan. But, at the same time, there has been a deep suspicion that Gorbachev will not last, an uncertainty about his durability. Third, there is a belief that negotiations with the Soviets should continue and be pressed. At the same time, however, there is a belief that extreme care should be exercised in those negotiations. Finally, there is a belief that while we should negotiate on arms reductions, we should not reduce our military power except in the context of carefully drafted and clearly understood agreements.

In sum, there is great optimism and there is great hope, but there also is a sense of caution about proceeding to a new relationship. Attitudes toward the Soviet Union in two years went from 45 percent favorable to an overwhelmingly positive 85 percent. This is a very volatile change, and it could be subject to drastic counterswings or reaction. It indicates that deep bitterness and anger could burst out if the optimism is not justified. The process of perceptive change is extremely fragile.

I would like to go beyond this question of perceptions, how we have come to these perceptions and what the percentages are, to a consideration of what is perhaps most important—the reality that freedom is stirring in the realm of our most formidable political enemy, our most formidable military potential adversary, the Soviet Union. The fact that freedom is stirring in Moscow has captured the attention and the imagination of the world. Even to the most skeptical among us, the Cold War seems to be ending. We are beginning to believe that it might be possible for the East and West to live at peace. For the first time in my experience, certainly since the end of World War II, it seems possible that the heavy burden of armaments that has been poised and ready to do battle to the death might be put aside. It seems possible that we and the Soviets will work on the constructive challenges of how to live in peace, rather than the major preoccupation of the past: how to avoid war or to prepare for war, or to go to war if deterrence fails.

FREEDOM, ELECTIONS, HUMAN RIGHTS

The stirrings of freedom to write, debate, and plan have brought significant changes, and those changes bring us great hope. The awakening of freedom in the Soviet Union has the effect of giving hope not only to the Soviet people, but also to us in the West. This newly emerging freedom creates untold opportunities. And we know also that this great powerful force will create unforeseen dangers.

We Americans, who live as free men and women, tend to measure the rest of the world by what we know that freedom and liberty have brought to us. And now we see that great quality we treasure and call freedom beginning to flourish in the Soviet Union.

Recently I observed elections to the Congress of People's Deputies in the Soviet Union. Implicit in an election is the freedom to choose one's leaders. It is a crucial, formal moment in the social contract between individuals and the society as a whole. It is a formal delegation, a legal transfer of power from individuals to rulers. Americans, of course, are election fanatics. An election is a metaphor of legitimacy for us, and we tend to measure the quality of others' democracy by how fair or how meaningful elections are in terms of bestowing power. We are interested in elections in Central America, in Korea, in the Philippines. We tend to measure the quality of democracy by how fair or how meaningful elections are. That is one of our measurements of freedom. So how do we, as Americans, evaluate the elections that have taken place in the Soviet Union? What were they like? I saw some of the polling places. The way that voting was set up, from what I saw, there was little likelihood of manipulation or of stuffing votes in the ballot box. No one has made a claim that there was much manipulation in the counting. From what I observed, there was a fierce determination and seriousness about the election. It was a very serious matter.

The campaign was not unlike a campaign in the United States. Many of the campaign speeches were broadcast on television, with time given to opposing candidates, including anti-government candidates like Boris Yeltsin. There was speaking on the streets, in the institutes, in the workplaces. There were posters all over Moscow, particularly in the case of Yeltsin, who was the most highly organized and who seemed to be the best financed.

I spent considerable time with five of the candidates who were running in the campaign and who were elected. The atmosphere reminded me of the period when I worked in the U.S. Senate. The Soviet candidates were calling campaign managers repeatedly, asking how the campaigns were going in various parts of their districts. There was much in the Soviet election process that was familiar. There was a sense of real contention and policy differences, certainly in those districts in which several candidates were running. Even in places where there was only one candidate—either because there was only one who dared to run, or where only one was permitted by the party apparatus—the people could exercise their vote in a negative way: a no vote counted. Under the Soviet system it takes a majority to be elected, so even a single candidate can lose if a majority of the votes is not cast in his favor, and this happened in a number of cases. Some major party bosses who were unpopular were defeated in that way. It was clear from the outcome of the elections that many votes were cast as a protest against the party apparatus. This is not to say that there was discontent expressed about Gorbachev, but there certainly was a desire to express opposition to the establishment. There were political sentiments in the air that Americans would recognize—"turn the rascals out," "it's time for change," "let's get some new faces."

From the point of view of freedom, the elections, which had sizable participation, present possible dangers. If the elected parliament does not have much significance, that recently aroused sense of commitment by the public will turn into anger, resentment, and apathy, perhaps worse.

As I have noted, Americans tend to regard elections as almost sacred, certainly as an inalienable political right, even as a human right. Aren't human rights, as we understand them, another one of those measurements for us of what constitutes real freedom? In the United States there is a strong legacy of human rights, but what is the Soviet perception of human rights? Is it basically different from what we regard as human rights? We have seen historically what Stalin's view was, and we have no use for that. We know that the Soviet constitution, for all its noble rhetoric, has not meant very much.

Let me cite Andrei Sakharov on the subject of human rights. More than any other individual, certainly for those of us in the West, he represented a test for the validity of human rights. Sakharov was sent by Brezhnev into internal exile in Gorky for his views. Among those views were forthright expressions of the lack of human rights in the Soviet Union. In 1987 I saw Sakharov shortly after his return from Gorky. It was the first time that I had met him. He had just been brought back from Gorky by Gorbachev. We both were attending a conference in Moscow on the global issues that face all of mankind. Those great questions included the ever-present danger of nuclear annihilation; the destruction of the planet's environment; the problems of poverty, disease, and underdevelopment, and human rights. I was present at the first exchange of views between Sakharov and Gorbachev. It took place in the Kremlin at a meeting of the board of the International Foundation for the Survival of Humanity, of which I am a member. There are members from the United States, the Soviet Union, and 18 countries throughout the world.

At the board meeting, one of our members, Academician Dmitri A. Likhachev, was asked to express his views to Gorbachev, and Likhachev turned to Gorbachev and said, "Mikhail Sergevich, we are here not just to talk about the question of human survival, we are talking about surviving in order to develop. Human development in this country, the Soviet Union, is not possible without leaders of great integrity. In the past we have not had leaders of integrity and we will not have development unless we have leaders who do. The ghost of Stalin and his kind was very much in the air." Gorbachev answered, "You are absolutely correct to say that. Our history is a sad one. We are only coming to know and fill in the white spots in our history. Terrible things happened in our country in the past. We were led by terrible men. Yes, you are right, *perestroika* and reform can only come if there are leaders of integrity. You are absolutely right." Whereupon Sakharov stood up and said, "I am glad Academician Likhachev brought this up, because it is indeed correct that we have been led by such men in the past. I have experienced directly their injustice and I want to say to you today, Mikhail Sergevich, that there is still injustice in the Soviet Union. I know because I have seen it with my own eyes." He then gave to Gorbachev 200 dossiers of people who he said were unjustly imprisoned. Gorbachev answered and said, "You are right to do that, and as a lawyer I know that the law lags behind the reality of society and that is why we have to change the law as we are changing all things in our country, and I will see to these cases." Of those 200, 197 have been released, and all political prisoners held under two notorious articles of the criminal code have been released. The possibility for investigating cases where there is a belief that there is imprisonment for political reasons or unjust reasons now exists. These are a few examples of the beginnings of the notion of human rights in the Soviet Union.

The Sakharov story is very important because he came to represent human standards in a number of respects. In 1968 he published a work in the West. It was circulated illegally in the Soviet Union as a *samizdat*—underground literature—with the title of "Progress, Peaceful Coexistence, and Intellectual Freedom." This work, which had a profound effect in this country and a profound effect on the nature of the debate on arms control, put forward a number of premises. The first premise was that before there could be any progress there had to be intellectual freedom. People had to be free to say what they wanted, investigate what they wished, and publish and speak freely. This was the root of political freedom. Without this there could not be any sensible arms control, there could not be any reasonable human development, and the great problems of war and peace, the environment, poverty, disease, and development could not be tackled. Sakharov was sent to Gorky for saying these things and for speaking the truth. Now Sakharov's views make up much of Gorbachev's platform. Much has happened in the Soviet Union since 1968, when to say such commonsense things was seen as subversive, and such writings had to be smuggled out to the West to be published.

REALITIES OF SOVIET SOCIETY

In the early 1980s the leaders of the Soviet Union began to recognize that things were going very badly in every respect—politically, economically, and culturally, as well as socially. General Secretary Yuri Andropov, when he had been head of the KGB, the secret police, had been receiving reports from his operatives, his people doing analyses, that the country was in a rotten state and that things had to be done. When Andropov became the general secretary of the Soviet Union, he began to discuss these matters seriously with the heads of institutes and the Academy of Sciences, and he called for research on these questions from the best thinkers in the Soviet Union. Notably, some of the best work was being done in Novosibirsk. Some of the people were there by choice, others were there by order. At any rate, one of the most influential efforts at Novosibirsk was a piece done by Tatiana Zaslavskaya, which is known to some in the West as the Novosibirsk Report.[2] This report addressed the question of what was the structure and reality of Soviet society, and why. Her analysis, which had profound effect because it paralleled the thinking of a number of key analysts in the KGB and in other institutes, made a comparison between the Soviet Union of the 1930s and the Soviet Union of the 1980s. Zaslavskaya said that in the 1930s, when Stalin imposed collectivization on the farms and severely limited all freedoms and pressed the nation into an all–out, almost wartime effort to transform the society from a backward nation into a modern industrial state, Stalin was able "to treat people as cogs in the mechanism of the national economy and the people behaved themselves just as obediently (and passively) as machines and materials."

However, in the 1980s, she wrote, Soviet society had been transformed from a peasant illiterate society into an urban, educated society, and the citizens of this new urban society believed that the purpose of the state was to serve them. "The level of education, culture, general information, awareness of his social position and rights has grown incomparably. The main body of

skilled workers on whom, above all, the effectiveness of the production process depends, nowadays has a rather wide political
and economic horizon. The socialist worker is able to evaluate
critically the leaders' economic and political activities, accurately
recognizes his own interests and can defend them if necessary.
The spectrum and needs and interests of workers is today more
abundant and broader than that of workers in the 1930s; moreover, in addition to economic, it includes social and spiritual
needs. It testifies to the substantial increase in the workers' personal development." That is a highly respected sociologist's
expression of the heart of the problem faced by the Soviet Union.
Her observations boil down to the facts that the political system
is resented, the economic system doesn't produce what people
want, and official culture is a sham. It is now evident that what
Zaslavskaya had written and what Sakharov had to say have been
accepted by the Soviet leaders. Their analysis has become the fundamental basis of the new thinking.

SOVIET NEW THINKING

What does "new thinking" really mean? Does the new thinking
really address the reasons for old myths and a path to new realities?
In analyzing their own society Zaslavskaya and Sakharov came to
the conclusion that they were part of a bankrupt political, economic,
and social system. But they looked around the world, as well, and
found a whole series of intractable problems that they were unable
to control.

From a philosophical point of view, Soviet thinkers regarded
this formidable array of problems and saw a whole group of issues
that could not be described in the classic formula of competition
between socialism and capitalism in which socialism, of course,
would provide the best answer. In the case of these issues, such
as the problems of nuclear weapons and destruction of the environment, an ideological finesse had to be devised. It was observed
that a new class of issues had emerged that Lenin and the founding fathers of the Soviet state did not recognize or were not able
to foresee, because these conditions did not exist at the time. And
these questions are clearly of such an order that they can only be
dealt with cooperatively; therefore, the highest premium is placed

on having peaceful, cooperative relations throughout the world. As a corollary, war in any form is too dangerous to have as a primary policy objective. Further, active peace, as they call it, is the highest priority, a new primary principle for Soviet international affairs. We can have some hope that the new Soviet foreign policy will have the stability and substance expressed in their new thinking and that we can proceed to work with the Soviets with this understanding.

INTELLECTUAL FREEDOM?

A very important element of intellectual freedom is the capacity to construct one's own sense of history. In 1988 in the Soviet Union no history examination was given upon completion of high school. This was an explicit admission that what the history students had been taught was false and that the whole issue of history had to be reexamined. They are trying mightily to fill in, as fast as possible, the so-called "white spots" of the past. The full enormity of the record of the Stalin regime—the millions who were murdered in one form or another, the great waste of resources, the brutal behavior of their leaders—is now coming to the attention of the ordinary Soviet citizen. There are people in the Soviet Union who have lived through the reality of the past. There are generations, too, who have not, and it is for them that history will have the greatest meaning, and it is for them that there has been the greatest shock.

Recently, I visited a cultural park in Moscow where there are museums and exhibits and entertainment—a kind of combination of the Washington, D.C. mall and Disneyland. There are more than 30 buildings dedicated to various aspects of human achievement. There are buildings for physics, for space, for chemistry, biology, etc. And there are also kabob sellers and ice cream and tens of thousands of schoolchildren. By chance, I wandered into a building labeled "philosophy." It was in the form of a great temple, and of course, inside there was Lenin in all his glory, with various portraits, sculptured busts, and an enormous number of posters. And then I saw a great crowd in a corner of the building and I went over to look. The crowd was staring at a group of posters with astonishment. On closer examination I saw a series of six posters about Stalin. One of them showed Stalin with a sharpshooter's rifle, and the target was a line of people facing a firing squad. Another showed a long freight train with faces peering through wooden slats looking like photographs of Jews being sent off to the gas ovens. The citations on the poster said at the top, "How many millions did he send?" The shock, the immediacy, and the power of those posters made an indelible impression on me. It seems to me now that it is very important for the Soviet people and the world to know the worst in order to bring out the possibility for the best.

How does one see whether there is freedom in the Soviet Union? You can't be sure unless you live there, obviously, but I have been able to visit frequently in recent times and to participate to some extent in ordinary life such as going to the movies. You can tell a great deal from the films now being shown. For example, I saw a film called "Is It Easy to be Young?" This was a Leningrad film about youth and some of their problems. It dealt with a group of young people who were on trial before a juvenile court because they had torn up a railway car after a rock concert. The bulk of the film had to do with the trial: the parents trying to explain the reasons for the actions of their children, the children explaining why they did these things. Much of contemporary concern found its way into the film—Afghanistan, the drug culture, the clash between generations, the issue of rock versus classical music, new clothing, wealth, the possibilities for a future with some value. There are also the films about Stalin, such as "Repentance," which came out of Stalin's own republic of Georgia. The films are, in essence, a condemnation and ridicule of Stalin.

There are many thoughtful films now being shown on the problems of youth, the problems of bureaucracy, the questions of authoritarianism. At many Soviet film theaters you might encounter a discussion period after the showing of the film. This was true at the showing I attended of "Is It Easy to be Young?" There was a great argument in the theater about what the film meant. The argument was presided over by a babushka who kept order and allotted time in a very correct manner. In fact, she put down one rather voluble filmgoer by saying, "Sit down, you have had your chance, be silent or you'll wear out your voice." They argued at length about the differences between the generations, they argued about Stalin, they brought out every element—aesthetic, political, or technical—that was in the film, and they did so without fear. That struck me as another sign of the beginnings of freedom. It was spontaneous and unrehearsed, and heartening to see.

CHANGING SOVIET LIFE

Other signs of the changes in Soviet life are the cooperatives—restaurants, car repair shops, etc. There is the famous case of the millionaire who made his fortune from the cooperatives. This millionaire has been the subject of great discussion in Moscow. It happens that the millionaire is a computer expert. He and a few of his technical associates formed a cooperative.Through their wit and imagination, they managed to buy, legally, quite a few computers and electronic equipment, sell them to state agencies and individuals below the cost the agencies normally would pay, and over a period of a year or so made a million dollars. And so the Soviet government was faced with the reality of having a millionaire who made money, legally, under the new system. Questions were soon raised, such as, what is a just profit? The issue of the right to be a millionaire was debated on television and in the papers. The majority opinion was that there should be a very steep progressive income tax.

Going to the market in the Soviet Union is still full of difficulties and hardships. Good food can be found in special markets where one pays twice the price. If one goes to the state market, one has to wait on line and may only be able to buy terrible food. Everyday life requires almost everyone to stand in a line for clothes, for shoes, for food. This is an aspect of Soviet life that everyone resents. There is a special way of walking in Moscow called the Moscow Trudge. This form of movement comes from standing in lines, pushing steadily (gently or not so gently) the person in front so that you can get closer to some goal. There is a sense that something important must be happening if there is a line.

Trudging aside, there are also signs of lively vitality. You see icons in abundance, religious art in abundance. There are experiments in all kinds of abstract art as well as the normal views of Moscow, Leningrad, and the various monasteries. There is also a great deal of poetry tacked up on the walls. On any given day on the *arbat* and some other market streets, you can see five or six poets declaiming, reading their poetry, and selling it for a few kopeks or rubles in mimeographed or hand-written copies. You can also see political campaigns, harangues of all kind, rock music as well as traditional music, punks and traditionalists. Outrageous avant-garde dress and costume abound. It is a very lively place. You can go to Pushkin Square on any given day and see either a demonstration in protest of the mistreatment of groups such as the Armenians or Georgians, or a celebration of the 1968 martyrs in Prague. Increasingly, these protests are allowed to go on, and with little or no interference.

What about television? What better way to control the minds and thoughts than through Soviet television. Yet, if you look carefully at television you will see that it has really changed in style and substance and has far more variety. Clearly, television from Western Europe and the United States has had an enormous influence. The Soviets now have something like "Good Morning America," which happens to be called "120 Minutes." They have the same pattern of anchor people, a man and a woman, the same time frames. For example, every few minutes news or comment will be offset by a bit of rock TV, a technique that is well known in the United States. There is pretty lively aerobic dancing and there is the news patterned on the U.S. model. Compared to the programming of a few years ago, there is now plenty of variety. The same is true of the evening programs. There is considerable on-the-street interviewing with questions like "What do you think of *perestroika*?" The people interviewed speak up directly, with little fear or uncertainty. A sports fan will find sports from all over the globe on Soviet television. For example, the Wimbledon tennis tournament and National Basketball Association games are televised. Every Sunday the Celtics or the Atlanta Hawks can be seen, or the games from the National Football League. There are talk shows and cartoons, including adult cartoons which are topical and which can be highly critical of government policies. Newspapers and other publications are also becoming interesting and lively. People now want to read them, and they are often sold out. *Moscow News, Ogonyuk, Izvestia, Literaturaya Gazeta*, the literary magazine, and many of the professional journals have much to say in lively prose.

FREEDOM AND U.S.–SOVIET RELATIONS

Some of this new vitality is the creative result of travel, foreign study, and exchanges. The opening up to the outside world is creating more ferment. This is contributing to the sense of freedom, and it is certainly contributing to the sense of variety. How does this impact on the U.S.–Soviet relationship? What do we do about this? Because the Soviet Union is moving in the direction of a more civil society, where human rights, political rights, and the idea of freedom, as we understand it, are all beginning to have more meaning, I believe that we can deal with such a country. Freedom is the necessary component for the change in the Soviet Union to have real relevance to us as a society.

We are now witnessing the blossoming of freedom in the Soviet Union. It may be that it is like "a thousand flowers blooming," as was the unfortunate case in China. But it might be a promising growth that can be sustained. In any case, what is taking place is certainly the greatest change in the Soviet Union in my lifetime. In the light of these changes and what would appear to be changed circumstances, it makes sense to work for a stable, long-term, peaceful relationship. We can be guided by the guideposts that the Soviets have imposed on themselves: loosening up their own society, deepening the sense of freedom, giving more value to human rights, moving their country to a more civil society, and engaging in the world in a way that can bring all of us a more stable and peaceful existence. What can we do about it? We should engage at all levels in talk and in exchange. We should try to understand what is happening and test all of these propositions to see whether there really is change. Ordinary Americans have the chance to see for themselves. In the past, only heads of state, diplomats, spies, and journalists were able to get some insight. Journalists certainly are seeing a much more diverse group of people now. Diplomats have far more freedom to circulate. Sovietologists have far more grist for their mill and far more material to work on—the archives are beginning to open. But people from all walks of life—physicians, ordinary tourists, students—have a great chance to see what is happening and to make their own judgments.

U.S. POLICY

If what is happening in Moscow is what I have described, what should our policy be? It seems to me that we should do everything possible to continue to reduce the tensions that exist between us. We should try to take advantage of the offerings from the Soviet side, to test them. For example, at the United Nations in December 1988, Gorbachev said that he would begin to reduce, unilaterally, 500,000 men. We should watch that process carefully. Six divisions amd several thousand tanks are significant numbers. It is quite possible that the Soviets will offer an additional increment, perhaps double that, in return for the reduction of several NATO divisions. The goal is to achieve a defensive parity at much lower levels. The question for the West, as it is for the East, is "Can stability be maintained at these lower levels? And if so, how?" And if there are going to be defensive forces that have little or no offensive capabilities, what kind of arrangements are needed for that goal? There are all real, active possibilities, and it seems to me that the U.S. government should press as hard as it can to see what is possible to achieve from these proposals. We should not delay unnecessarily.

In the past it has been argued by some policymakers that we should not trade with the Soviet Union, that we should not offer credits, because it would help the Soviet economy and contribute to a military force aimed at world domination. Trade should be on the basis of mutual interests. If it is good for our business and it doesn't place our country in jeopardy, or weaken security of the West, we should encourage trade and commerce. We should now examine very seriously the question of credits, the issue of the Soviet Union joining the economic world order, the possibility that there will be a convertible ruble. Where will these opportunities begin? We know that there has been a very small amount of trade between the United States and the Soviet Union. Trade in the past was limited by the non-convertible difficulties of the ruble, not to mention the difficulties of the Cold War. There have been proposals to create an economic free zone in Armenia, including convertible rubles. There are proposals for the development of a new kind of energy generation, small steam-injected gas turbines, the possibility of small chemical plants, earthquake-proof prefabricated housing. There is a whole range of new commercial trading possibilities.The Soviets seem to be interested in turning their collective farms into small family farms. This is an area where the U.S. experience could be of value. There could be much that the Soviets could learn, and there may be considerable money to be earned by assisting the development of small farming in the Soviet Union.

We should continue to expand exchanges of peoples in every field of human endeavor in order to increase understanding, knowledge, and critical judgment. If we look to the United Nations, we see that for the first time the Soviets are an active partner in that international forum. New proposals have been made by the Soviets suggesting that the Security Council peacekeeping might, in fact, for the first time, be a reality. Cooperation between the Soviet Union and the United States is certainly possible on matters of terrorism, narcotics, and crime. And on regional issues we have already seen the beginnings of different Soviet attitudes, as reflected in the withdrawal from Afghanistan, the change in Angola, the possibilities of rapprochement with China, the opening of relations with the conservative Arab states, and even the beginnings of some dialogue on Central America and Cuba.

Finally, then, what does this all mean for us? Does freedom have the same—or recognizably similar—meanings to us as to the Soviets? This is the key question. If we consider what Jefferson in the eighteenth century thought freedom was, is it the same as we think freedom is now? What about the French revolutionaries in 1789? What about Khomeini and his freedom? What about the freedom of the Russian revolution and Stalin?

We all know that a change is taking place in the Soviet Union. We have a fairly good idea of what is happening, and we have the means to monitor it. What we are witnessing is a society in crisis, a society that is moving, however tentatively, toward becoming a more civil society. As an American, I hope that movement continues. It is in our interest. And if it is to continue, it is going to require leaders—not only in the Soviet Union but in the United States—of great courage and wisdom, and it is going to require the support of their peoples.

NOTES

1. The text of NSC–68 can be found in Thomas E. Etzold and John Lewis Gaddis, eds., *Containment: Documents on American Policy and Strategy 1945–1950* (New York: Columbia University Press, 1978), pp. 385–442.

2. The Novosibirsk Report was extensively quoted in the *New York Times*, Aug. 5, 1983, p. 1. See also Tatiana Zaslavskaya, "The Novosibirsk Report," *Survey* 28 (1) (1984): 88–108.

4

New Myths in Soviet–U.S. Relations

Vladimir O. Pechatnov

We speak of "old myths and new realities," but myths need not
necessarily be old in order to be out of touch with the realities.
Indeed, as I will argue, new realities themselves may give rise to
new myths, while some old myths of Soviet–U.S. relations—like the
myth of the monolithic Soviet bloc or the irredeemable nature of
the Soviet system—are disappearing. Sometimes the old myths re-
surface in a new disguise, adjusting in this peculiar way to the new
realities.

Of course, it is hard to be totally scientific in separating myths
from reality; it is all rather subjective, one person's realities are
often someone else's myths and vice versa. So I will offer a personal
view of what I think are the new (and sometimes not so new) myths
in Soviet–U.S. relations, myths persisting mostly, but not exclu-
sively, on the U.S. and Western side.

The first of them deals with the origins of *perestroika* and new
Soviet foreign policy in particular. It may be called the "we brought
it all about" myth. It exists in different forms, ranging from rather
sophisticated to very crude ones, but the basic logic remains the
same: it has been Western pressure, the patient and consistent
containment of Soviet power, that has successfully frustrated the

Kremlin's "global design" and forced the Soviet Union into a reappraisal of its "expansionist" policies.

SOURCES OF *PERESTROIKA*

This view does not hold water conceptually, since it ignores the decisive domestic sources of *perestroika* and reduces its external aspects to mere response to the U.S. pressure, whereas the new thinking originated in a far broader and deeper context of longtime learning and adaptation to the changing global environment. As for the effect of "containment," at least an equally good case may be made for the opposite thesis: namely, that militarized containment has actually contributed to the ossification of the anti-American policies on our part, while a more accommodating posture has led to their relaxation.

But my main problem with this interpretation has to do with its misleading policy implications. For if this pressure is what makes the Soviets act, then the recipe is very simple: maintain and even increase the pressure and you will get *new* results. Some even see it as the best way to help *perestroika*, if not Mikhail Gorbachev personally. According to this "the worse the better" logic, the more difficult is Gorbachev's situation, the more likely are really radical reforms as the only way out of the crisis. What can be said about this view? Let me be clear: *perestroika* is not primarily about pleasing the West and improving our image abroad. It is something that we are doing for ourselves.

The Soviet people need and deserve democracy and human rights. We need the emancipation of society from the bureaucratic bondage at home and the opening of society to the rest of the world abroad. If this happens to be to the liking of the West, that is "O.K." with us. But we will continue on this road anyway, whatever the West does, although appreciation and support would, of course, be more helpful than increased pressure.

Another related, but somewhat older, myth is that the Soviet Union needs détente, especially arms control, badly, much more so than the United States—especially now, because the Soviet Union is in such a mess internally—and that it can be made to pay almost any price for that. This view holds that in the West you should keep your powder dry, not take anything at first offer, and that the Soviets will come around with new, unilateral steps, offering more valuable concessions and gifts. This may be sound commercial advice, but what is good for horse-trading is not necessarily good for much more complex international politics.

THE COLD WAR AS A "GOOD" THING

Contrary to this viewpoint held by some in the West, opportunities are never consistent; they are not something that you can put in your savings account and then use sometime in the future. In history opportunities come and go, and the art of statesmanship, to a large degree, is an ability to seize them in time, before they go away. They may go away not just because Gorbachev, despite all his political skill, cannot endlessly afford to come up with new, unreciprocated, unilateral steps. The opportunities may also diminish because time is running short for both of us. Beneath the surface of tranquillity, problems and challenges are piling up, and it is in our mutual interest, not only in the Soviet interest, to get rid of the burdens of the Cold War and to start dealing with real problems.

And that brings us to another bit of today's conventional wisdom, especially fashionable among strategists and realpolitik proponents. I am referring to the notion that the Cold War was actually a blessing, or at least a very useful thing. There is almost a nostalgia for the Cold War in some quarters. Such nostalgia may seem to be premature, but it is also understandable since the Cold War *is* really fading away. There is some logic to this mood: during the Cold War there was the tested method of maintaining the semblance of world order after World War II by means of the bipolar rivalry, of dividing the world into confronting blocs headed by the two preponderant military superpowers. It was a crude but functional device, which could be credited with maintaining the "long peace" and was also good for the egos of the two superpowers.

These "benefits" of the Cold War system are now being compared to the possible consequences of its demise: eventual breakup of the alliances, fragmentation of the world, "Balkanization" of Europe, anarchy and chaos everywhere. The implied conclusion is simple, although not widely publicized—"If it ain't broke, don't fix it." Preserve as much of it as possible for as long as possible.

This view of the Cold War as a good thing is vulnerable on at least two important accounts. First, it ignores, or at least downplays, the darker side of the picture, the price that has to be paid by our two countries and the rest of the world in order to maintain that system in place. That price was especially high for the Soviet Union and for the United States. Consider the economic price of the arms race and the inversion of national priorities—building up these huge military arsenals while other nations were building up their economies. We have exhausted ourselves in this rivalry, and now we are paying for that dearly in our debts, our budget deficits, our falling competitiveness with other nations, our unmet social needs.

There was a high political price, too—obsession with national security and abnormal expansion of national security establishments in both countries. The influence of the Cold War on U.S. political life is well known. It goes beyond McCarthyism, since even after that the political climate, in part because of the "Soviet threat" and the Cold War, remained far more hospitable to the right wing and conservative forces. This helped to exclude left and liberal alternatives from the U.S. political process.

The story of the Cold War in Soviet life and of its political impact within the nation is still largely to be written. But it is quite obvious that the damage was even greater than it was in the United States. To put it in a few words, it helped to prolong the life of the Stalinist system, providing external justification for it. The Cold War also distorted our thinking about ourselves in the world, militarized and simplified it, and made us blind to much of what was really going on in the world. As Senator Fulbright noted 26 years ago, quoting from David Riesman, the Cold War was "a distraction from serious thought about man's condition on this planet."[1]

So much for the notion of the Cold War as a good thing.

But there is another false presumption in this myth and its implications—namely, that the Cold War structure of the world *may* be preserved. A number of long-term irreversible trends are undermining that structure. The world is becoming more diverse, multipolar, and interdependent at the same time. It is less susceptible to military and unilateral solutions. Therefore, our ultimate challenge is not to preserve the artificial cement of the Cold War or to substitute it with a "better" (as some people think) form of superpower hegemony—Soviet–U.S. condominium, but to adjust to these global trends and to find a new way of organizing world order, based not upon bipolar hegemony, military power, and counter-vailing blocs, but rather on true multilateralism and new mechanisms of international security and cooperation.

To lead the rest of the world toward this new order, to help to shape it while both of our countries still possess the exceptional shaping power (a situation that would not last much longer) should be, in my view, our next joint and much more noble historic mission in this world.

PERESTROIKA'S PROSPECTS

Another current myth, which hinders our joint efforts in this direction, deals with the purposes and prospects of *perestroika*. It pictures the latter as another Soviet exercise in strategic deception aimed at using the breathing spell of the new détente for refurbishing Soviet economic and military power, which then would be used against "the deceived and demobilized West" in a renewed strategic offensive.

In response to that, I would say, first of all, that we want—both unilaterally and reciprocally—to drastically reduce the military component of the national power and ultimately to exclude the use of military force from international relations. And our recent actions in this sphere have proved that these are not just good words and benign intentions.

Yes, *perestroika* is clearly undertaken for revitalizing Soviet society and for increasing our prestige and influence in the world. And no major reform movement in history was ever launched with different purpose in mind. But given our current predicament and the whole meaning of *perestroika*, we can become stronger only if we become quite different—much more open, pluralistic, and democratic, far more closely integrated into the world community.

That in itself would create a whole new set of domestic constraints on the exercise of the state's power both internally and externally. The combination of hostile isolation from the rest of the world with a huge military machine and almost total freedom of using it had been at the core of not only the "Soviet," but well before that the "Russian," threat as perceived in the West by such different people of different times as Friedrich Engels in his *Foreign Policy of Russian Tzarism* and Paul Nitze in the "NSC–68." *Per-*

estroika and the new thinking are transforming all of these equations simultaneously, making the Soviet Union safer for its own people and for the rest of the world. If successful and reciprocated, they would change the very nature of the traditional East–West relationship.

A TURNING POINT

This, finally, leads me to another current fictional image of the Soviet Union as a "grand failure," a system that went bankrupt and is beyond repair. Ironically, we have unwillingly contributed to the emergence of this image ourselves by our merciless self-criticism and by blunt exposure of what went wrong in our country. But if we look at the picture more calmly and objectively, we will see that the rumors, of our death, as Mark Twain put it once, are "slightly exaggerated."

Of course, the crisis is there, but to begin with, crises are an inevitable and even necessary phase of development for any society, through which it adapts to the new environment. In this sense, *perestroika* may be rightfully seen as not only a sign of weakness, but of strength, and of new self-confidence as well. Our present political leadership is the first in many years that feels strong and secure enough both at home and abroad to undertake unprecedented reforms in domestic and foreign policy and to let many of the formerly unthinkable things happen.

Also, this is the crisis of one specific type of socialism—"barracks-style socialism" of Stalin's model (which was hardly socialistic at all)—and a painful and strenuous search for a different model—a truly democratic and humane socialism.

People such as Zbigniew Brzezinski keep saying that this is impossible, that truly democratic socialism is a contradiction in terms. That reminds me of Stalin's peculiar logic with its familiar refrain, "It is impossible because it can never be possible." But who can say for sure? It still has to be proved as well, of course, that there can be a synthesis of socialism and democracy. After all, that is what *perestroika* is all about. It is a great experiment in realizing socialism's potential, a collective journey of discovery. It is still too early to predict its outcome, but like many of our people, I do hope that in the not-so-distant future these times will be seen as a turning point in the redemption and rehabilitation of socialism, which is, after all, a very noble idea, born in the West.

MAKING THE WORLD SAFE

But, ultimately, the point is not who will prevail in this competition of different ideals and social systems. On this history will be the judge. Our task is different—to make the world safe, but safe not for U.S. capitalism or for Soviet socialism, but for diversity, as President John F. Kennedy used to say, and for the coexistence of different ideals and social systems, their learning from each other.

The great ideological schism between socialism and capitalism is becoming increasingly irrelevant to the real problems that we face individually as nations and collectively as humankind: disarmament, protection of the human habitat, prevention and settlement of regional conflicts. We have come a long way from the heyday of the Cold War, but it may be a sad commentary on our times that Senator Fulbright's call of a quarter of a century ago still has not lost its meaning—to convert the Cold War into a "safer and more internal rivalry, one which may be with us for years and decades to come, but which need not be so terrifying and so costly as to distract both of us and other nations of the world from the creative pursuits of civilized societies."[2]

NOTES

1. J. W. Fulbright, *Old Myths and New Realities* (New York: Random House, 1964), p. 137.
2. Ibid., p. 16.

5

The Cold War in Transition

Joseph L. Nogee

In recent years, there has been a debate among academicians, government officials, and journalists as to whether the changes brought about by Mikhail Gorbachev have ended the Cold War. Margaret Thatcher some time ago declared the Cold War to be over. On the other hand, National Security Affairs advisor Brent Scowcroft questioned whether it is over. The academic community has been divided. George Kennan says yes it is, as do Stephen Cohen, Richard Ullman, Robert Legvold.[1] Those taking a more cautious view included scholars like Seweryn Bialer, Michael Mandelbaum, and John Lewis Gaddis, to name a few.[2] The *New York Times* recently editorialized that "The Cold War Is Over." Asked at one of his early presidential press conferences whether he thought the Cold War was over, George Bush responded, "I wouldn't use the term."[3]

There is little doubt that during the past few years U.S.–Soviet relations have moved toward a détente, and that on the whole this is a desirable development. What is the nature of this new détente? We have gone through phases of tension and conflict alternating with peaceful coexistence and détente before. The question is whether the change under Gorbachev is simply another phase in the superpower relations or something more fundamental. I will attempt to identify what I believe to be the major causes of the

Cold War, assess some of the existing obstacles to the termination of the Cold War, and then conclude with suggestions as to what it would take to end the conflict.

CAUSES OF THE COLD WAR

The Cold War is the longest war that either the United States or the Soviet Union have ever fought. Obviously, such a protracted conflict did not result from any single event or even from the policies of any one administration. I would argue that the causes of the Cold War go beyond the policies of Joseph Stalin or any single development such as the communization of Eastern Europe. The causes of the Cold War are complex and multiple, and they operate at several different levels of analysis. Three impress me as being particularly important. First, there are geostrategic considerations that derive from the balance of power. Second, there is the conflict between the Soviet political system and its political future and that of the United States (and the West in general). And third, perceptions and misperceptions of the elites and publics of both sides have contributed to the conflict.

Geostrategic Considerations

The Cold War began in the aftermath of World War II as a result of an imbalance of power that was created in Europe. Germany as a great power was destroyed. Britain and France, though victorious, emerged weakened from the war and were unable to play their historic role in Europe's classical balance of power. There was, in short, a political vacuum, which the Soviet Union moved aggressively to fill. This threatened to bring about Soviet domination of Europe and led almost automatically to a U.S. response to balance Soviet power in Europe. Twice before in this century the United States had gone to war in Europe in order to prevent Europe's domination by any one single power. In the post–World War I period U.S. involvement was motivated essentially by balance-of-power considerations. This fact, for one thing, explains why there was no Cold War before 1945, notwithstanding the fact that the Soviet Union was a Communist state ruled by Joseph Stalin. As the

United States and the Soviet Union emerged from the war as great powers they inevitably became rivals.[4]

The policies pursued by the United States to check Soviet expansion, what became known as the policies of containment, are classical examples of the kind of balance-of-power politics that have been pursued by great powers since the beginning of the nation-state system. These policies included the North Atlantic Treaty Organization, the Marshall Plan, the Truman Doctrine, and the arms race. The Sino-Soviet alliance in 1950 and the Korean War made the balance-of-power rivalry global in scope. Thus, one major factor behind the Cold War was the bipolar international structure that emerged in the post-war period. The United States and the Soviet Union would have become rivals as great powers no matter what the domestic political makeup of the Soviet Union had been. Eventually, of course, the territorial struggle tended to stabilize and the contest for a global balance took the form of an arms race in strategic nuclear weapons between the superpowers.

Russian Soviet Political Culture

A second cause of the Cold War was the Soviet political cultural and its conflict with Western and U.S. values. Those elements of the Soviet political culture that I am referring to involve its tendency toward expansionism, its suspicion of the outside world, and its obsessive security-mindedness. The roots of this political culture go far back in Russian and Soviet history. Indeed, there are many factors that contribute to this political culture. There are what might be called Russian factors, ideological factors, and Soviet factors. Before the revolution the Russian state had a long history of conflict with its neighbors. Russia has, over the centuries, been invaded often by Western and non-Western powers. This produced in the Russian political culture a deep sense of insecurity and a profound suspicion of the outside world. It has contributed to the growth of autocratic institutions in Russian political life, which some historians have argued have been necessary in order to build and preserve the Russian state and to maintain its territorial integrity.[5]

The advent of the Bolsheviks to power in 1917 brought a new dimension, an ideological dimension. Communist ideology has had the effect of reinforcing traditional Russian views toward the outside world. Bolshevik doctrines tend to emphasize the adversarial nature of relations between the Soviet Union and non-Communist world. The core values of Marxist—Leninist doctrine stress the notion of politics as conflict. With Marx it was class conflict; with Lenin, the conflict between imperialism and socialism. Another aspect of the ideology is the utopianism of socialism, which has tended to reinforce traditional Russian messianism. Now, I am not arguing that ideology dominates Soviet thinking today, for clearly that is not the case. I am suggesting that some of the core ideas of that ideology have influenced and reinforced the Russian political outlook, particularly that which focuses upon the notion of politics as conflict.

Another ingredient of the Soviet political culture is what I call the Soviet element. The Soviet system, as it has evolved up to this point, is unique. It is neither Russian nor Marxist. If one label had to be applied I think the best would be Stalinist. It is a unique type of authoritarian system that, although it may be undergoing change, still retains many of the essential characteristics of the pre-Gorbachev period.

One of the problems of the Soviet system from its inception has been the issue of legitimacy, creating for all Soviet leaders a degree of insecurity. There are many ways by which governments and regimes can acquire legitimacy. Traditional Russian monarchy based its right to rule on God and the principle of divine right. Democracies base their legitimacy on popular sovereignty as expressed through elections and other democratic procedures. Until now the Soviet leaders relied on neither of these two. The two major sources of legitimacy in the Soviet system have been ideology and performance. The doctrines associated with Lenin define the Communist Party of the Soviet Union as the legitimate political organization to rule and hold power in the Soviet Union. The problem with reliance on doctrine as a basis of legitimacy is that as people cease to believe in the ideology the legitimacy of those who hold power based upon it is undermined.

Another source of legitimacy is performance. On this score the record is very mixed. Probably the single most important factor contributing to the legitimacy of the Soviet leadership was the success of the Soviet Union during World War II in preserving the state and protecting the country against the Nazis. Victory in World War II unquestionably added more to the legitimacy of Stalin and the Soviet leadership than any other single factor. That was followed by the acquisition of nuclear weapons. The Soviet Union became a great power and then a superpower, all of which contributed to the authority of those who ruled the Soviet Union. On the other hand, balancing the successes in foreign policy has been a mixed record in domestic accomplishments. In recent years Soviet performance in the domestic arena has been appalling, thus undermining the credibility and the legitimacy of Soviet leaders.

Elite and Public Perceptions

A third factor contributing to the Cold War has been elite and public perceptions of each other. We know that there have been enormous distortions and misperceptions on both sides. There has been a tendency for each to create a kind of a devil image of the other. Western misperceptions have been well known. The misperception of Roosevelt at Yalta in his first post-war encounter with Stalin is an example. The phenomenon of McCarthyism in the United States is an example of how distorted the perception of an adversary can become.

The fear that developed in the United States after the Soviet Union orbited its Sputnik that Soviet science had overtaken U.S. science was unfounded. Other U.S. misperceptions of the Soviet Union concerned the missile gap, the bomber gap, and the myth of monolithic Communism. So, on both sides, this problem of myth construction about the other—its capabilities and intentions—contributed to the underlying tension of the Cold War.

FUNDAMENTAL CHANGE?

To sum up, the Cold War was the product of a number of forces. Those that I have mentioned are only the most salient; there are others. At one level there was the geostrategic struggle to maintain a balance of power, at another the aggressiveness and suspicion of the Soviet political culture, and yet at a different level, misunderstanding on the part of political elites on both sides.[6] Now the question is, Has this all changed? Has Gorbachev wrought such a fundamental change in U.S.–Soviet relations that we can now think of the Cold War as a thing of the past?

Let me repeat my contention that the Cold War did not come about as the result of any one political leadership. If that is true, then it seems likely that it will require more than one administration to make a permanent change in the superpower relationship. The détente of the past few years is very important, but it has yet to end some of the fundamental points of conflict between the United States and the Soviet Union. Let me point out an important feature of the Gorbachev record that is sometimes overlooked.

We associate the great change in Soviet politics with one man, Mikhail Gorbachev. It is, however, important to note that Gorbachev's record is a mixed one and that in the early period of his administration (1985–86) there was a basic continuity in Soviet foreign policy from the previous administrations. There was no significant break at all. In Afghanistan, for example, Gorbachev did not set about to end that war, but rather to win it. In the period 1985–86 he substantially increased Soviet forces in Afghanistan and changed in a very brutal way the character of that war. His oft-quoted description of Afghanistan as a "bleeding wound" reads in full, "counterrevolutionaries and imperialism have turned Afghanistan into a bleeding wound."[7] The implication, of course, is that the crime was committed by China and Pakistan (counter-revolutionaries) and the United States (imperialism), not the Soviet Union. Then there was the tragedy of Chernobyl, which generated a great deal of bad feeling between Moscow and Washington and for a time made a mockery of Gorbachev's posture of *glasnost*.

The first two summit meetings between Reagan and Gorbachev were contentious and involved on both sides the kind of maneuvering for position that had characterized some of the previous summit meetings during the height of the Cold War. There was the Daniloff incident when a U.S. journalist was seized by the KGB in exchange for a genuine Soviet spy. Also, Soviet political rhetoric in this period was strident and intensely anti-American, consistently condemning the United States as being on the wrong side of every political issue throughout the globe. A particularly nasty illustration of that propaganda was the Soviet accusation that the AIDS virus was a CIA concoction for use against the peoples of the Third World.[8]

SOVIET POLICY SHIFTS

The change in Gorbachev's foreign policy took place early in 1987. We can only speculate on the factors that determined the cause and timing of that change, but in retrospect it seems likely that the January plenum of the Central Committee of the Communist Party of the Soviet Union played a critical role. It would be interesting to be privy to the debates that went on leading up to that plenum, to know who argued what and when precisely the important decisions were made. We know that this was an extremely heated session because that Central Committee meeting had to be postponed twice. In the January plenum Gorbachev admitted that his initial efforts for *perestroika* were not producing results. He acknowledged the depth of the problem confronting Soviet society and the Soviet economy and the need not just for reform but for radical changes throughout Soviet society. Quite likely Gorbachev had come to the conclusion that there would have to be a fundamental change in U.S.–Soviet relations if the extensive political and economic reforms he envisioned were to have a chance for success.

Also important to the shift in Gorbachev's policy were the changes made by the Central Committee in the membership of the ruling organs of the party, the Politburo, and the Secretariat. Two holdovers from the Brezhnev period were ousted and three supporters of Gorbachev, including his close ally Alexander Yakovlev, were taken into the leadership. This strengthened Gorbachev's working control over the higher party organs, the organs that are still the critical center of decision making in Soviet politics.

Events moved quickly after the January plenum. Within a month of the meeting Gorbachev announced the first of what were to be a series of changes in Soviet foreign policy. On February 28, 1987, he stated that the Soviet Union was ready to consider an agreement on intermediate-range nuclear forces (INF) completely separate from space weapons and strategic weapons. And he followed that up shortly thereafter with acceptance of the zero option and the zero–zero option and acceptance of on-site inspection to monitor compliance with an INF agreement. Later, during 1987 and 1988, Gorbachev made the commitment to and the withdrawal of Soviet forces from Afghanistan. Also, during 1988 and 1989 he showed a willingness to reduce Soviet commitments elsewhere in the Third World. Another step toward détente was the December 1988 announcement of a significant unilateral cut in Soviet military forces. These and other policies demonstrate a consistent and determined effort to build an improved relationship with the United States and the West in general.

REMAINING PROBLEMS

What, then, are the remaining problems before there is likely to be a broader consensus that the Cold War really has ended? I will identify a few that remain. I do not believe that the United States and the Soviet Union yet have a common vision of what kind of a world each state would like to help bring into existence. I believe we continue to have different visions of what kind of a world order is desirable.

The United States seeks an international order in which legitimacy rests on conformity with democratic processes and societies that are essentially pluralistic in their political structure. The Soviet Union remains committed to one-party regimes based upon some variation of Marxist–Leninist principles. The United States seeks an international economy where international trade and exchange are based upon market principles, and the Soviets seek a global economy with exchanges between state-controlled economies.

There has been a great deal of talk about the modification of Soviet ideology, about the decline of ideology in the Soviet policy. However, if you look at Gorbachev's statements made for domestic consumption, you will find that notwithstanding some significant modifications, reflected in the "new thinking," Gorbachev has hardly renounced Leninism or Lenin's distinction between imperialist and socialist regimes. It is difficult to define exactly what part ideology does play in Soviet thinking or how to assess it, but Gorbachev has yet to abandon the basic and underlying principles of Marxism–Leninism.

I interpret the essence of Gorbachev's new thinking to be the argument that the primary goal of foreign policy must be the avoidance of nuclear war, a position with which most of us would agree. But that in itself is not new. Nikita Khrushchev made that same point in the 1950s with his ideas on peaceful coexistence. If you look at those countries throughout the world with which the Soviet Union has the closest political and economic relationships, you see countries that are either Marxist regimes or very anti-American in their foreign policy. In Africa: Ethiopia and Angola; in Asia: Vietnam and North Korea; in the Middle East: Libya and Syria: in Latin America: Cuba and Nicaragua.

The Soviet Union may be in the process of disengaging from some of its involvements in the Third World because it is finding (as the United States has learned) that involvement in the Third World is difficult, costly, and often unproductive. But the Soviet Union has not abandoned any of its clients. Indeed, Gorbachev, even through 1987 and 1988, consistently either maintained at a high level or increased military and economic assistance to major Soviet clients in the Third World. In 1988 the Soviet Union provided $1.5 billion to Angola, and it provided approximately $1 billion in military and economic aid to the Sandinistas in Nicaragua. As for Cuba, the Soviets have for a number of years been supplying military and economic assistance at around the level of $5 billion annually. Even by Soviet standards that is a very large sum of money. What Soviet interest—beyond a competition with the United States—is served by subsidizing the Cuban economy by that amount of money?

THE FUTURE OF EUROPE

Another problem that must be resolved before we can genuinely talk about the end of the Cold War is the division of Europe. This is, of course, where the Cold War began, and despite important changes, the issue has yet to be resolved. It was not settled at Helsinki in 1975 with the Helsinki Agreement because of the basic fact that the peoples of Eastern Europe, over 100 million in number, were not represented there. From the time the Berlin wall was erected in 1961 through early 1989 more than 600,000 Eastern Europeans have fled to the West. That figure does not include the scores of thousands of East Germans who began the mass exodus from East Germany in 1989, leading to the fall of the wall.

The point here is that the peoples of Eastern Europe have clearly not accepted as definitive and final the political, social, and economic order imposed upon them in the Stalin period. One might ask, What is the justification for continued Soviet military presence in Eastern Europe today? Is it security? I do not think that that it is arguable today. A non-nuclear Germany is no threat to the Soviet Union. Is it economics? Stalin ravaged these areas, but for many years now the economies of Eastern Europe have been a drain and a liability on the Soviet economy. Is it ideology? To some extent that may explain Soviet concern. If Communism is displaced across the border, as appears possible, it will certainly be undermined where it began. Also, there is a Soviet fear that self-determination for the peoples of Eastern Europe could threaten the internal order of the Soviet Union itself. After all, if the Poles, Hungarians, and others can be self-governing, many nationalities in the Soviet Union will seek the same prerogatives. The Latvians, Estonians, and Lithuanians clearly want independence now, and there are stirrings for autonomy in the Ukraine and in the Caucasus.

Finally, I think the geopolitical factor is still important. The fact remains that the United States and the Soviet Union have arrayed against each other an arsenal of weaponry capable of destroying the other. Even in a time of change, the Soviet Union remains militarily the strongest power in Europe, and the balance in Europe is preserved only by NATO and the commitment of the United States in Europe's defenses.

ENDING THE COLD WAR

Despite these obstacles to normalization of relations, I do not believe that the Cold War is interminable. The end will not come quickly. It will be a protracted termination whose beginning we may have been witnessing. The conditions that will bring about that final termination follow from the arguments made previously. These conditions would include a substantial disarmament in Europe and the dissolution of the North Atlantic and Warsaw Pact alliances. There must be a sharp reduction in strategic nuclear weapons, particularly those that have a first-strike capability. Nuclear abolition is likely to remain unattainable although nuclear stockpiles can be reduced to much lower than existing levels for deterrence to remain effective. Sharp reductions in nuclear weapons and their delivery systems are going to be necessary before either side can feel a genuine sense of security.

Another requirement for normalization is self-determination for the peoples of Germany and Eastern Europe. The division in Europe created in the 1940s was artificial and, as has been increasingly apparent, never became rooted in the European consciousness as a permanent fact of political life. Additionally, both sides are going to have to find a strategy for promoting development in the Third World on the basis of indigenous social forces and not through regimes imposed from the outside. Moscow is going to have to abandon completely its imperial ambitions, not simply modify its tactics.[9] And finally, *perestroika*, or some variant of Gorbachev's vision, must take hold in the Soviet Union before there can be a genuine end to the Cold War.

NOTES

1. See Richard Ullman, "Ending the Cold War," *Foreign Policy*, no. 72 (Fall 1988), and Robert Legvold, "The Revolution in Soviet Foreign Policy," *Foreign Affairs* 68, no. 1. The *New York Times* published a series of op-ed articles on the topic "Is the Cold War Over?" in January-March 1989.

2. See John Lewis Gaddis, "The Evolution of US Policy toward the USSR in the Postwar Era," Michael Mandelbaum, "Western Influence on the Soviet Union," and Seweryn Bialer, "The Soviet Union and the West: Security and Foreign Policy," in Seweryn Bialer and Michael Mandelbaum, eds., *Gorbachev's Russia and American Foreign Policy* (Boulder, Co.: Westview Press, 1988).

3. *New York Times*, April 2, 1989, p. E30.

4. Adam B. Ulam, *The Rivals; America and Russia since World War II* (New York: Viking Press, 1971).

5. Arnold Toynbee developed this thesis as follows:

The pressure on Russia from the West did not merely estrange Russia from the West; it was one of the hard facts of Russian life that moved the Russians to submit to the yoke of a new native Russian power at Moscow which, at the price of autocracy, imposed on Russia the political unity that she now had to have if she was to survive. It was no accident that this new–fangled autocratic centralizing government of Russia should have arisen at Moscow: for Moscow stood at the fairway of the easiest line for the invasion of what was left of Russia by a Western aggressor. The Poles in 1610, the French in 1812, the Germans in 1941, all marched this way. Since an early date in the fourteenth century, autocracy and centralization have been the dominant notes of all successive Russian regimes

Civilization on Trial in the World and the West (New York: Meridian Books, 1953), p. 238.

6. These factors are discussed more fully in Joseph L. Nogee and John Spanier, *Peace Impossible—War Unlikely: The Cold War between the United States and the Soviet Union* (Boston: Scott Foresman, Little Brown, 1988), chap. 8.

7. Mikhail Gorbachev, "Political Report of the CPSU Central Committee," in *Current Soviet Policies IX, The Documentary Record of the 27th Congress of the Communist Party of the Soviet Union* (Columbus, Oh.: The Current Digest of the Soviet Press, 1986), p. 35.

8. Subsequently Moscow acknowledged the falsity of that accusation.

9. For a thorough and up-to-date study of Soviet involvement in the Third World, see Alvin Z. Rubinstein, *Moscow's Third World Strategy* (Princeton: Princeton University Press, 1989).

6

The Continuing Dilemmas of Soviet Reform

Timothy J. Colton

In his classic book, *Power and Policy in the U.S.S.R.*, Robert Conquest likened the Kremlinologist to the paleontologist, who exhumes and examines the calcified bones of extinct species. There was much to the analogy: not only was the Soviet system ossified in crucial respects, but the evidence we could obtain about power and influence was scarce and, all too often, denatured. Today we are being forced to think and work much more like physiologists, who examine living, adapting organisms. The advent of Mikhail Gorbachev allows us and challenges us to examine our methods of study and our deeper assumptions about what counts in Soviet politics, about what is conducive to chance, and about the limits of change.

Any discussion of Gorbachev must begin with the nature of the Soviet predicament as of his assumption of power. The Soviet Union's ailments may be sorted into two rough categories, which we might label those defined by "situational factors" and those imputable to "structural factors." On the former set, there is no need to belabor the obvious. The Brezhnev leadership long overstayed its time in office, running out of energy, a sense of purpose, and credibility with the population. Leonid Brezhnev's death in November 1982 was followed by an interregnum in which first one and then a second interim leader attempted to make an impact but was kept from accomplishing anything much by health and other limitations. In March 1985, when Gorbachev took office from Konstantin Chernenko, there was a gathering sense that the country had drifted for too long and that something had to be done about emergent problems.

The weightiest of these problems, as Gorbachev was soon to acknowledge, rested on the institutional foundation of the Soviet regime, most of it laid during the rule of Joseph Stalin, from the late 1920s to 1953. Soviet reformers, Gorbachev included, now speak of the stalinist model as a "command-and-administer system"—"*komandno-administrativnaya sistema.*" Like all gross generalizations, this one is too glib if taken literally, but it is a useful starting point. The Soviet Union has a command economy, based on the principle of control from above; one might stretch the concept a bit and speak of a command polity. Stalinist command structures were modified and somewhat humanized under Nikita Khrushchev, but after 1964 Brezhnev and his coterie essentially accepted them as they were and made do with minor adjustments within them.

The stage was set for Gorbachev by the growing gap, from approximately the mid-1970s onward, between inertia-bound leaders and institutions on the one hand, and the dynamism of Soviet society and of the broad environment of politics on the other. In economics, the highly centralized state machine was increasingly ineffective in the age of high technology, as Gorbachev now has stated emphatically, and was hard pressed even to maintain previous levels of performance in areas of old technology, including one as old as agriculture. Partly because of the past modernizing successes of the regime, Soviet society was more complex, more resistant to direction and manipulation, and more demanding of its government. In political life, an urban and educated populace had less use than before for ritualized participation and for other carryovers from a simpler age, such as the farcical cult that surrounded Brezhnev's personality in his twilight years.

None of this is to say that the Soviet people were taking to the streets in outrage. Far from it: the typical reaction was one of alienation and of what has variously been typified as "inner emigration" and "privatization" of concern and effort. Gorbachev was confronted not with a rebellious citizenry, but with disengagement, apathy, and ennui.

If Soviet society was in a kind of uneasy slumber, Gorbachev's first response after March 1985 was clear—to set off an alarm bell that would wake everyone up. He did this in his early months in power partly by being physically vigorous, punctual, and forceful, thereby contrasting sharply with the decrepit leaders who preceded him. He launched a bloodless purge of the Soviet elite, pensioning off thousands of veteran officials, corrupt and honest, and replacing them with younger, more patient, and generally better qualified individuals. Only two months into his term, the government moved to ration the alcohol supply, a move calculated to demonstrate its seriousness about arresting social decay. In the economy, Gorbachev called for redirection of resources toward the development of advanced technology, especially in the civilian sector. He also came out for *glasnost* in the official media, meaning greater publicity and candor about Soviet shortcomings.

LINES OF ADVANCE

As an initial response, these decisions were a welcome change from the torpor of the previous decade, but they were hardly a wholesale assault on the status quo. The surprising thing about Gorbachev has been his shift toward more fundamental changes. When I wrote the second edition of *The Dilemma of Reform in the Soviet Union* in 1986, Gorbachev was beginning this maneuver. After first indicating that the patient, the Soviet system, needed only to be sobered up, cleaned up, and limbered up, Gorbachev soon started to say that it really needed surgery, and drastic surgery at that. In short, Gorbachev set off down a considerably more radical path in 1986 and 1987. The main lines of advance can be encapsulated in three words: *glasnost, perestroika, demokratizatsiia*.

About the first, I can be brief because the main facts are well known in the West. Gorbachev and his allies carried out lightning raids in the mass media, firing Brezhnev-era editors and bringing in younger and more modern media managers. Censorship of the printed word was greatly relaxed, though not eliminated. There was a commensurate thaw in television, filmmaking, and most of

74 74   U.S.–Soviet Relations

the other arts. The leaders called for empiricism and honesty in scholarship, especially in economics and the social sciences. As a corollary, they assented in a startling wave of reinterpretation of Soviet history, far more sweeping than the first round of de-Stalinization under Khrushchev.

Gorbachev has used *perestroika*, the second leg of the triad, mostly to encompass economic renovation, although he also employs it as a summary term for his reform effort. Economic *perestroika* embraces a number of specifics, among them a streamlining of central planning, a devolution of some administrative functions to the level of the firm, and an acceptance of some market principles and of what Gorbachev now describes as "the laws of the market." Perhaps more important in the long run, the Gorbachev leadership has given its blessing to the emergence of a private and "cooperative" sector, which has been anathema to the Soviet Union since the New Economic Policy of the 1920s, and also for experimentation of hybrid forms of ownership, such as regulated joint-stock companies and arrangements for leasing of state enterprises by managers and workers.

In social and socioeconomic policy, Gorbachev has unveiled a series of initiatives, especially in the three subsectors of housing, health care, and the food industry. In each case he advocates an acceleration of state effort and a transfer of resources from other pockets, including the military budget.

As for *demokratizatsiia*, political "democratization," Gorbachev championed it only in January 1987, after almost two years in power. A special 19th Party Conference in the summer of 1988 agreed in principle to make serious changes in political institutions. Since concrete measures are still in the process of being implemented, it is difficult to know what their actual impact is going to be.

POLITICAL CHANGE

It is not too early, however, to note some early effects and trends. Most exciting, in the light of the Soviet tradition of bogus elections, have been the multi-candidate elections tried out for 1,500 territorial seats in a new Congress of People's Deputies in the spring of 1989. In many parts of the country these produced sharp clashes and resulted in the defeat of conservative-minded candidates. Electoral reform feeds into legislative reform: here, the new line calls for legislative bodies at all levels to emancipate themselves from their executives and to provide effective forums for the airing of grievances and the thrashing out of policy. The Supreme Soviet, the national assembly selected by the deputies' congress, is now of workable size (with about 550 members, versus the 1,500 it had before 1989) and is to have active committees and to sit for six to eight months a year.

Gorbachev is committed to several other political reforms of great potential moment. One is to reduce the interference of the Communist party apparatus in the operations of governmental organs, partly by slashing party staffs and dissolving most of the apparatus's divisions for branches of the economy. Another is to introduce a degree of democracy within the party itself, where competitive elections of leaders, subject to check from higher levels, have become fairly common. Yet another innovation is the promise to overhaul the Soviet federal system and to give the 15 ethnically based republics real rather than nominal rights vis-à-vis the center. Then there is the idea of instituting what a motion adopted at the 1988 party conference dubbed a "socialist state of law," which might loosely be translated into the Anglo–U.S. phrase "rule of law." The practical measures being contemplated here include legislation clarifying the position of the press, giving the courts greater independence, augmenting the rights of the accused (to defense counsel, for example), removing some especially onerous punishments (such as penal exile), specifying the powers of the KGB, and greatly shortening the list of crimes against the state.

Perhaps most encouraging, there seems to be a genuine change of heart within the political leadership and within most segments of the Soviet political elite about the need to accept a far wider and more differentiated spectrum of opinion and expression than has hitherto been condoned. Gorbachev now speaks glowingly of "socialist pluralism." The modifier, "socialist," suggests that there are limits to the heterogeneity he is contemplating, but the more important point for the moment is the embrace of pluralism, a Western concept that until recently was a term of scorn in Soviet discourse.

The strongest signal that the ice was breaking was the decision in December 1986 to free Andrei Sakharov, the leading dissident of the Brezhnev era, from internal exile in Gorky, a decision that Gorbachev conveyed in a personal telephone call to Sakharov. This was followed within months by the release of most of those still imprisoned on blatantly political grounds. As this unfolded in 1987 and 1988, the regime also telegraphed its willingness to moderate its long-standing hostility toward unofficial, voluntary associations unattached to the state and party. Soviet sources now speak of 60,000 such "informal organizations"—Soviet citizens know them by the abbreviation neformaly—with combined membership of several million persons. Many of them deal with matters as innocuous as stamp collecting or bird watching, but a large subset do have direct or indirect involvement in politics. The regime has promised that it will shortly enact a new statute on mass organizations, which will legitimize many of them but is also likely to try to impose certain limits on them.

Now that the authorities are reconciled to the existence of such entities, they are learning to tolerate activities previously beyond the pale—of which the most remarkable example is that of public assembly and demonstration. I spent some weeks in Moscow in the summer of 1988, around the time of the 19th Party Conference, and the political change that I had the greatest difficulty getting acclimatized to was in this area. Stroll through the streets and squares of central Moscow, and you would find petitions being signed, knots of people arguing about Stalin or Sakharov, rallies, displays of political theater and satire—far more public-motivated action than you would come upon in the typical Western capital. And the range of issues and proposals drawing comment was mind-boggling: everything from the restoration of the Romanov dynasty to anarcho–syndicalism, Western liberalism, evangelical Christianity, and animals' rights.

GRAND GESTURES AND TRADE-OFFS

Without question, a good deal has happened since March 1985. On many dimensions, the change in perception and thinking has been little short of revolutionary. And, it should be stressed, this has not been the work of one man alone. Gorbachev is not a lonely hero fighting impossible odds. He has sought and built elite and mass support for most of what he has done.

All the same, no one, least of all Gorbachev himself, would argue that things have gone smoothly or that reform has become, as he has proposed numerous times, "irreversible." A key problem from the beginning has had to do with trust in the process of change. This is not the first time the Soviet people have been promised improvements, in the economy and elsewhere. The fact that past hopes have been dashed has made many Soviets wary of the siren call of *perestroika* this time around. Soviet citizens are also aware that the tendency in Soviet history has been for the political pendulum to swing between reform and conservatism. Were the normal rhythm to assert itself when Gorbachev dies, retires, or is removed, it would not be unreasonable to expect a swing to the right. This worries many who might otherwise be enthusiastic about reform, and without whose investments—in, say, a long-term lease in a farm or restaurant cooperative, or a legislative committee—reform will be doomed. Gorbachev has been alert to this problem. It probably accounts for his proclivity for grand gestures, to convince his audience that his commitment to reform is authentic and to create a bandwagon effect.

A second dilemma facing Gorbachev involves the trade-off between ambiguity and clarity. Any observer would be hard pressed to pin down precisely what Gorbachev is trying to accomplish. He wants to reform the system, this is obvious. But how far does he intend to go? Is he willing to reform the Soviet order out of existence, if that is what is takes to deal with its problems? There are no ready answers to such questions. In part, this is because Gorbachev and his colleagues have groped their way forward from one issue to the next—discovering, as he has put it several times, that Soviet society is like an onion, from which the leaders peel back one layer of problems only to discover another beneath it.

Lately, Gorbachev has become visibly perturbed about adverse reaction to this stepwise approach. In January 1989, in a meeting with editorial and media personnel, he declared, not terribly convincingly, that there is an overall strategy for *perestroika* and that he and key members of his Politburo team, like Prime Minister Nikolai Ryzhkov, were already thinking up the strategy before Brezhnev's death. Despite this assertion, he was unable or unwilling on this and other occasions to articulate just what a duly reformed socialism would be like. This lack of a crisp vision of the future, understandable though it may be, inevitably reinforces the mistrust of skeptics who fear that his reforms will lead nowhere and that anyone implicated in them will pay the price.

CONFLICTS AND CONTRADICTIONS

A third kind of contradiction has been among the respective goals of the leaders themselves. In the economic realm, for instance, the regime has been saying since the party Central Committee plenum of June 1987 that it is going to combine market and planning coordination, retaining the latter in essential ways while introducing the former and reaping its fruits. While such an amalgam looks feasible in theory, experience elsewhere shows that it has been exceedingly difficult to achieve in practice. Eastern European reformers have been struggling with the puzzle for two decades in the case of Hungary and for almost twice as long in Yugoslavia; many of them now seem to be concluding that it is insoluble and that the best way forward is to institute a regulated capitalist economy, such as Poland and Hungary are now committed to doing.

Another illustration comes from political reform. Gorbachev wants what he calls "democratization," yet he insists in the same breath that this cannot mean, at least while he is leader, multi-party democracy of the Western type. He is thus stuck with growing tensions—within the Communist party, which is still the only legally recognized political party, and between it and other social forces, such as the burgeoning mass movements in the Baltic republics. The fact that the Soviet Union resigned itself in 1989 to moves toward Western democracy in much of Eastern Europe is likely to worsen these tensions.

Another contradiction is expressed in disagreement among individuals and groups rather than merely among objectives. It is vital to recognize that Gorbachev presides over a coalition of disparate reformers, united only in their rejection of Brezhnev-style "stagnation," but disunited over many other matters, large and small. At the party conference in 1988, Soviet television viewers were treated to the unfamiliar spectacle of Igor Ligachev, one of the most conservative members of the Politburo, engaging in open polemics with

Boris Yeltsin, a fellow ally of Gorbachev's but politically well to his left, who had been ejected from the Politburo only a few months before. Intra-coalition conflict on a grander scale has occurred over the issue of inter-ethnic relations, an enormous subject which I can only make passing reference to in these remarks. Here, local nationalists who came to the fore under Gorbachev's aegis have drawn up secessionist platforms that are bringing them into collision with the central Soviet state and with Gorbachev himself.

Two additional contradictions in the reform process merit consideration. One might be termed the antagonism between disorder and order, or between disintegration and reintegration. Any epoch of great reforms must begin with a dismantling of key parts of the old system and then proceed at some point to an assembly of new institutions. Gorbachev, it must be said, has been a genius at disassembling elements of the pre-existing Soviet system but not nearly so adept at fashioning something to take its place. This point applies especially well to economic performance, where an already laboring central planning mechanism has been subjected to new strains and has shown signs of breakdown in the consumer sector, but little by way of a substitute market system has made an appearance to date.

A related contradiction is between promise and performance. In his first several years in power, Gorbachev enjoyed a predictable period of grace. Now that the honeymoon is over, he finds the public much more demanding than before—and it is he, after all, who has exhorted the population to expect more from its rulers—and, on the whole, distinctly ungrateful for what he has so far wrought. Many Soviets are starting to ask the question posed so devastatingly in the 1984 Democratic primaries in the United States: "Where's the beef?" Sooner rather than later, Gorbachev must deliver some of the beef he has promised or else pay the consequences.

LINKAGES WITH FOREIGN POLICY

Let me turn to the linkages between internal reform and foreign policy. The Soviet Union in 1985 was not short of foreign policy problems: a mini-cold war with the United States, a rusting empire in Eastern Europe, a futile war in Afghanistan. These problems, to be sure, paled before those on the domestic order. They also presented Gorbachev with opportunities to score quick successes, if need be, by making out-and-out concessions to foreign adversaries. And this, by and large, is what he has done in foreign relations, on issues from arms control to Afghanistan and Eastern Europe.

In the long term, the domestic and foreign agendas are intimately interbraided. Prodded by Foreign Minister Eduard Shevardnadze, a close ally of Gorbachev (and the only member of the 1980 Soviet leadership, except for Gorbachev, still to be in the inner circle), *glasnost* has affected foreign policy as well as domestic politics, if not yet to the same extent. Parliamentary commissions on foreign policy and national security have begun to query diplomats and generals in ways unthinkable until now.

The Soviet Union's defense burden, to take the most obvious of the specific points of commonality, handicaps them in dealing with their domestic economy. It is thus no accident that Gorbachev has begun to prune the military budget and to direct the savings to investment and consumer needs. The economic woes, to turn the problem around, more and more hobble the Soviet Union in selling the attractiveness and even the viability of Leninism and state socialism abroad. So economic renovation, whether successful or not, is bound to have implications for the Soviet Union's place in the world, and Gorbachev will push it in no small part for that very reason. The Soviet Union's traditional autarchy from the international economy is one prime reason for its lagging growth and backwardness, and this isolation must be addressed if economic reform is to proceed. Early decisions on liberalization of foreign trade procedures, direct foreign investment through joint ventures, and participation in international economic institutions show, at a minimum, that the Gorbachev administration is cognizant of the interconnection and is determined to proceed on both fronts.

The general thread running through these specifics is encouraging for Western interests: provided Gorbachev or someone like him continues to lead it down the trajectory started in 1985, the Soviet Union will be more conciliatory, more commercially inclined, and markedly less of a menace to our physical security. While it has all the flaws to be expected of any human invention, Gorbachev's *perestroika* is a step in the right direction for the world as well as for the Soviet Union.

7

U.S.–Soviet Relations: Problems and Promise

Karl W. Ryavec

Clearly, the U.S.–Soviet relationship has been quite significant for U.S. society and politics. The United States is a different country now partly because of the existence of the Soviet Union as a perceived problem or even threat. The United States became a world-scale military power because the expansionist power of the Soviet Union prevented the full demobilization that always followed America's wars.[1] Americans have not dealt adequately with certain of their problems (e.g., the deterioration of the economy, or the rise in social problems) because of their preoccupation with Moscow.

Ironically, other problems have been somewhat alleviated because of the fear of being embarrassed by Soviet propaganda. For example, a study of black American soldiers in World War II claims that Harry Truman desegregated the army in 1948 because the old U.S. army was too easy a propaganda target for the Soviets. In any case, partly because of the Soviet Union, this country is governed a bit more responsively than it would otherwise be. Capitalism today strives to avoid embarrassment and conflict. Perhaps the Polish communist who said, justifying Soviet-type communism, that "At least, we have civilized capitalism," has a point. Or do we just have here two unrelated phenomena in the same time frame?

BASIC ASSUMPTIONS

My main assumptions are four:

1. There will be some mutual unease and even friction between the United States and the Soviet Union for a long time. We are very different, after all, despite a current mutual desire to get along. But these differences will not lead to war.

2. The Soviet Union and the United States are not enemies; they are rivals or competitors, but not in a total sense.

3. There is no relationship worthy of a name between the two (i.e., it is a relationship of little content and substance).

4. The Soviet Union is still expanding in international influence, but this process is not inherently aggressive or radically oriented; Soviet power has still not reached its high point, but the increase in Soviet power will now take place as part of the normal foreign policy of a great power that accepts the international system and the "rules of the game."

PROBLEMS

There exist a number of perennial or at least recurrent irritants and problems in U.S.–Soviet relations.

On both sides these are:

1. some emotionalism and even fear;

2. a sense of difference and puzzlement at one another;

3. the recurrence of turbulence and "ups and downs" (e.g., we always ask for or expect too much from the Soviets and then we are annoyed and reject them when they do not deliver).

On the U.S. side we note:

1. unease at the lack of political rights and the repression of dissent (even now, under Gorbachev, state censorship continues); people are still detained for their political activities, and 50 to 100 people are being held in special psychiatric hospitals for political or religious reasons;[2]

2. the huge size of the Soviet military (Gorbachev has promised us only a 10 percent cut, which may well improve the Soviet military machine,

and he continues the deployment of new weapons systems (e.g., launching two new aircraft carriers in 1989);

3. Soviet support of anti-American governments and movements and Soviet "spoiling" operations in the Third World as well as anti-American propaganda and disinformation.

On the Soviet side there are:

1. annoyance at the "volatility" and lack of clarity and consistency in U.S. politics and the U.S. inability to agree to a significant military step that would increase Soviet security (we are still, despite the INF Treaty, about where we were ten years ago in strategic arms control, the key to a truly improved relationship);
2. fear of U.S. high-tech weaponry;
3. U.S. support, though mostly verbal, for liberalization in the Soviet Union and especially in Eastern Europe;
4. annoyance at the cultural attractiveness of the United States and the poor light in which this puts the Soviet Union.

NON–PROBLEMS

Although the Soviet mood on all this has "lightened up" under Mikhail Gorbachev, the concern has not disappeared. Yet it is crucially important to note that the United States and the Soviet Union have never had certain serious problems come between them that have troubled the relationships of other states:

1. territorial or border disputes, as between Japan and the Soviet Union;
2. the desire for revenge for a past injury, as between France and Germany between 1871 and 1945;
3. the tensions from having lost part of one's people to the other, as between Romania and the Soviet Union;
4. a history of war, as between the Arabs and Israel;
5. contention over valuable resources.

What, then, is at dispute or at least at the bottom of the dispute, for certainly the U.S.–Soviet relationship is a contentious one even if it is somewhat cooperative, at least recently?

THE DISPUTE

Basically, the central problem of the United States and the Soviet Union is wrapped up with World War II, the way it ended, the post-war world that emerged, and particularly the new, non-contentious, relatively prosperous, middle-of-the-road and suburbanized America that emerged after 1945, as well as the consolidation of a new elitist industrial society by inhuman Stalinism in the Soviet Union and its growth in power through the acquisition of territory and allies, both willing and unwilling.

Neither the post-war United States nor the Soviet Union were able to deal with each other, since each was the one remaining threat to the new power and the novel internal arrangement that World War II had brought to both. The main victors had seemed to overcome their earlier problems. The United States seemed to be at peace with itself (no more leftism and no more class conflict) and, in the Soviet Union, a system that ought to have fallen apart or been eradicated because of its mass murders and imprisonment of millions had reversed 700 years of German history. "Success" had been achieved. The Soviet system had proved, by beating back German fascism, that it had a right to exist. It may even have earned a real degree of acceptance from at least its Russian population. For the first time since the 1200s the "East" seemed to be moving West.

Yet, neither system was complete in its victory; each was reminded of its limitations and artificiality by the other. Accordingly, they had to be in conflict. It was unavoidable. Both systems were then too distinctively different to cooperate. But, ironically and significantly, neither superpower offered a total challenge to the other. Despite the unpredictability and the tenseness of the Cold War, each opposed the other only in a limited way, a fact that is apparent only now with the benefit of 20/20 hindsight. Deputy Secretary of State Lawrence Eagleburger, who has suffered derision in the press and has been overruled in Soviet policy by his superiors, is undeniably correct in general in saying, "For all its risks and uncertainties, the Cold War was characterized by a remarkably stable and predictable set of relations among the great powers"[3]

In effect, in 1945 the United States and the Soviet Union "ran into" each other's advancing power without either one being prepared for the encounter. The Soviet Union was not prepared to deal with the United States as a world power because that result seemed so unexpected and out of character for the United States (remember Roosevelt's statement to Stalin at Yalta).[4] Also, because the Soviet Union was so badly damaged by the war, it could not compete with a United States that had just doubled its gross national product between 1941 and 1945 and that also had the atomic bomb, which it had used.

The United States, for its part, lacked the requisite experience of being a great power and, more important, was unable to deal coolly with having an opponent. This may still be true, as our recent experience with Castro, Khomeini, Qaddafi, Noriega, Ortega, and others suggests. All our past opponents either went away (the British) or were made to go away (the native Americans). The Soviets and the Americans were (and are?) ill-matched as well as fated to fear and threaten one another. If East Central Europe had not come under Soviet domination or if the United States had returned to isolationism, there might not have been a Cold War. Likewise, if colonialism had not begun to disappear at the same time and had not created a fractions and turbulent unclear international context of insecure regimes, nationalism and ancient hatreds becoming foreign policy, both superpowers might not have been drawn into regional conflicts, causing them to pretend they were enemies.

It once did seem just possible that the Soviet Union could begin to cut off the United States from those foreign natural resources it needs to maintain its unique style of life. The former Soviet pretense of being revolutionary, coupled with the Third World's demand for weapons and its image of revolution, supported U.S. fears.

This, added to the fundamental differences in U.S. and Soviet culture as they affect politics, economics, and society, drove both superpowers to continue World War II, but now against each other, long after it could have ended. Anti-Nazism was "converted" into anti-Americanism there and into anti-Sovietism here, and the two military industrial complexes, developed to face the German challenge, found a reason to stay in existence through a new, though usually cold, war.

GORBACHEV AND THE UNITED STATES TODAY

Now we are in a new ballgame, or so it seems. The Cold War is over, not because one rival bested the other, but because both have tired of the chase and the challenge, and are considering, though only considering, concentrating on their own internal difficulties and unfinished agendas and fostering stability in the world, if only by benign neglect. Both superpowers have recently been cooperating in East Central Europe, one allowing and the other fostering Poland's, Hungary's, and perhaps even East Germany's development of democracy and the market. Ronald Reagan did not, even with his foreign-supported deficit-producing monster defense budgets, make the Soviet Union cry "uncle." It would have been more intelligent—and cheaper—to have waited until the Soviet elite realized, as it largely has, that the Soviet Union must change in some general if not fundamental way in order to remain a viable country into the fast-approaching twenty-first century.

Gorbachev is a unique individual, but even without him something like a milder *glasnost* and *perestroika* would have emerged, though they would have been blander and less exciting. Reagan's defense budgets were wasted. The Soviets did not force the Americans back to the western hemisphere or make them give up their interventionist capabilities and inclinations. No one "won" the Cold War. It simply was neglected as it was replaced in both countries by real problems—serious environmental degradation, loss of productivity, and that real societal malaise Jimmy Carter was rash enough to mention. (Although a case can be made for the United States as victor in the Cold War, based on recent developments in Eastern Europe, we must note, in opposition, that the Soviet Union has not had to allow the changes that have taken place there. Its decisions to do so are part of a broad, new policy that was established because of significant political changes in the Soviet Union.)

Still, despite the new détente between them, neither has yet changed in fundamental nature. Each remains unique in its own way and retains those features that once drove it into the Cold War. History could go backwards—or at least mildly so—if certain domestic or foreign policy events were to erupt, and given enough time, they will. The inscription on the National Archives building in Washington is: "The Past Is Prologue." When a taxi driver in Washington was asked what that meant, he answered, "You ain't seen nothin' yet!"

We may have only a limited amount of time before this unreal peace in U.S.–Soviet relations is threatened, if not disturbed or destroyed, although no "new Cold War" is likely. We both lack the stomach for that.

The new international environment, although it shows cooperative and democratic tendencies, is not secure and certainly not one the superpowers can control. In addition, economic dynamism and high-consumption societies have developed elsewhere, particularly in Japan and Western Europe. The recent failure of both superpowers to win wars in the Third World has seriously undermined their military credibility and has encouraged aggressive tendencies in other countries. Consider the Syrian invasion of Lebanon. For example, what occurs in East Central Europe in the next few years and in the Baltic republics will be a real test for the Soviet Union and for U.S.–Soviet relations. The United States may be similarly tested in Mexico and Central America. Even though the Soviet foreign minister has said his country is willing to negotiate an end to the Warsaw Pact if NATO is also eliminated, it beggars belief to think the Soviet Union would not continue to exercise significant influence over Eastern Europe and not attempt to keep the Baltic republics inside the Soviet system. As Eduard Shevardnadze has said, "These states do not cease to be our neighbors, friends, allies."[5]

Gorbachev and his change of direction has struck Americans as a most welcome harbinger of "détente as we would like it." Certainly, anyone who has been in the Soviet Union recently or who has dealt with visiting Soviet faculty or students thankfully recognizes that a real change of mood has occurred in the Soviet Union—so much so that the way things were there can never be fully restored, a viewpoint that is emphasized by some Soviet citizens one meets.

The U.S. jazz musician Louis Armstrong was once asked, after he toured the Soviet Union, what he thought about the Russians. He considered this question for a while and answered, "If the Russians would only relax, they would be all right." Well, they have relaxed, at least to a point. But these same relaxed people also tell you: (1) Gorbachev may not succeed, and (2) economically, things are getting worse, not better. An October 1989 opinion poll in *Ogonyok* revealed that only 12 percent of the Soviet population feels *perestroika* will lead to significant economic improvement, while 23 percent said their standard of living had worsened over the past year. "Chronic scarcity has given way to a critical sense of deprivation."[6] As David Cornwell, alias John le Carré, puts it so brilliantly, "The Reconstruction was not yet a visual medium. It was strictly in the audio state."[7]

The Soviet system is bigger than Gorbachev. And he is a confident political manager, not a democrat, a Soviet political Lee Iacocca but without Iacocca's practical business and industrial experience. It is exciting to read about Gorbachev and perhaps inspiring to see and hear him speak, yet there is no evidence he can get the Soviet bureaucratic machine and the working class to work better and produce higher quality goods. Still, there is no denying Gorbachev has learned how to manipulate U.S. cultural proclivities, such as faith in change and trust in certain types of personalities, to his and the Soviet Union's advantages. As a visiting American was told in the Soviet Union a few years ago, "We are going to make it impossible for you to dislike us." Soviet Americanists and Gorbachev make a good team. The Bush administration has been forced to respond with words of acceptance and promises of aid unimaginable in the past. But, as Andrei Sakharov put it, Gorbachev is "improvising" and trying "to achieve democratic change through non-democratic means . . . an extremely dangerous strategy, threatening to bring forth unworkable anti-democratic structures we'll have to live with for a long time."[8] Gorbachev is even beginning to make despot-type utterances, as when he suggested in the fall of 1989 that the editor of a newspaper who had published a poll with unwelcome news for "number one" to resign.[9] In addition, at least two peaceful demonstrations in 1989 were dispersed with brutal force, one in Tbilisi and the other in Lvov.

The French have a word for this: "Bonapartism," or "plebiscitary democracy." Note that the new Supreme Soviet that will make the laws is elected indirectly by a body in which the Communist Party controls at least one-third of the seats. This is a significant step toward democracy, and maybe this is all the Soviet elite will allow, but it is not democracy. For most Americans, the case for democracy is built upon placing a high value on the rights of the individual to choose and expel from office his and her leaders, the "all men are created equal" for politics argument. The second argument, not made often here, is the one a contemporary Machiavelli might produce: democracy allows the ruling class, as long as it knows how to win elections, to rule without serious "interruptions" and with the advantages of having correct knowledge of what's going on among the "masses." It is this "safety-valve-and-*glasnost* democracy" for which Gorbachev argues, not the one based on individual rights. I say this without being one of those "conventional" Sovietologists whom Alexander Yanov criticizes as "imprisoned by their decrepit dogmas" into a blind anti-Sovietism.[10] Good analysis, however, demands that we specify as exactly as possible what Gorbachev is doing and not fall victim to the hopes and fears of either the past or the present. We must also ask the right questions even if we cannot answer them.

One such question is: What does the power structure want from Gorbachev, and what does it not want from him? I doubt that the elites want a free society unless it is clear they could retain their privileged positions in it. Some could, of course. These would tend to follow Gorbachev. But as a young Soviet academic told me, most people who say they are for *perestroika* are just trying to hitch their wagons to the victor. When they get the positions they want, they will turn on those who are really for *perestroika* and tame or destroy it. Part of the working class may also be opposed to *perestroika*. Some Soviet workers in various areas of the Soviet Union have expressed opposition to the free market and also to greater power for minority peoples.[11]

In any case, there are limits to *perestroika*. Some of it has not yet occurred and some of it has already been reversed. Collectives of doctors have been put out of existence, for example. As Natan Sharansky (Anatoly Shcharansky) tells us, "Many dissidents have been released..., but repression, persecution and political prisons have not disappeared.[12] Neither have "psychoprisons," as a group of visiting U.S. psychiatrists found.[13] Independent publishing is still not allowed. A cynic might say, paraphrasing the famous last line of the film "Casablanca," that the unofficial slogan of *perestroika* is, "Release the usual suspects." "The KGB remains in place as a privileged agency," Nicholas Daniloff reminds us, and it is one that Gorbachev is using to push his policies and protect him.[14] Certain U.S. scholars who were in the Soviet Union in March 1989 report that KGB representatives requested they report to them any Soviet official who said he was opposed to *perestroika*.

Perestroika is not yet a clear result but still a developing stage in the life of Soviet society. It is a statement, not a program, and definitely not the beginnings of democracy. Change will be a long-drawn-out and possibly tragic and even bloody process taking generations. Gorbachev himself has said significant change will take generations. Many people in the Soviet Union do not accept pluralism and are not prepared to deal calmly and non-violently with certain issues. The Soviet Union must return to the stage of 1917 in some respects and start over. Régis Debray has made a similar point. Gorbachev has, perhaps unwittingly, begun a new process of modernization by the "renewal of tradition."[15] We have even seen a Soviet foreign minister say, "We violated the norms of human behavior; we went against general human values."[16] Although unavoidable, such a freeing of the repressed past is a threat for a multi-ethnic state in which little assimilation has occurred and in which "Soviet" is not an ethnic category. The Soviet army has had to negotiate with a minority people's organization to get supplies to Armenia, and developments in Estonia proceed to the point where an Estonian currency is discussed in public while the Russians, who may be Gorbachev's ultimate nationality problem, are divided by class, politics, and geography.

Gorbachev is creating what might be called a "French bureaucrat's democracy," that is, a place where almost anything may be published or said, but where the administrative elite—or a small faction within it—continues to make the decisions on its own. Gorbachev is saying, "Tell me, people, what you want so I can decide what is best for you." At most this is a healthy, self-confident authoritarianism. But historically, such systems do not outlive their creators. Russia has had many reforms over the past 300 years but it has always remained recognizably Russian (i.e., a highly centralized and bureaucratized governmental system in which society is weak and individual rights are limited). Despite *glasnost*, there has been no substantive change in the Soviet institutional structure or in the processes and principles with which government operates. The pluralism Gorbachev advocates is the one-party limited variety. Can a pyramid become a Parthenon by draping it with democratic symbols, the dissident writer Andrei Sinyavsky asks? Until *glasnost* extends to the inner errors of the Gorbachev administration and *perestroika* restructures the "basic Soviet model" of government and society, political change is limited and may be rolled back, if only partly. Gorbachev is personally secure, particularly after the Politburo changes of September 1989, but his program is not. He captured dominance within the elite only to find that the elite is a stagnant force, one without positive controls or catalytic properties. It can only reign supreme and protect itself, not renew the Soviet Union. Only new forces, not yet dominant, might carry out Gorbachev's *perestroika*. And they might well want to do it without him.

CHALLENGE OF RESTRUCTURING

Economic restructuring will be Gorbachev's great test. And here he may fail, at least in his lifetime. He is a brilliant politician, but making people work efficiently to produce high-quality, exportable goods is not something a politician can accomplish. It might be satisfying to be on Gorbachev's staff, but he offers no firm hope for the people who do the work, be they bureaucrats or entrepreneurs. The Soviet Union is far behind China in economic reform. There, more than 40 percent of industrial production comes from non-state industry.[17] Even so, China ran up against serious domestic contradictions, not yet resolved.

Is what we see what we get? True, Gorbachev has begun a mood change that will begin to erode the rigidity of Soviet government, but economic reform demands changes in economic principles, organization, and process. Impediments to economic change must be swept away as well. Entrepreneurs must be able to borrow money, retired people in business must able to keep their pensions, local officials must be induced to allow businesses to begin and flourish, prices must be made more realistic, and so on. Can Soviet society accept this? Can Gorbachev accept it? Will the peasantry develop its economic role? The general director of an agro-industrial kombinat laments that "there is no economic lever which could induce a peasant to engage in trade."[18] Has Gorbachev arrived too late? We must be realistic about the near-term results of *glasnost* and *perestroika*. They are welcome, they are good for Soviets, for Americans and U.S.–Soviet relations and the world in general, but they cannot provide what many Americans want. *Glasnost* is not democracy. *Perestroika* is not a Soviet economy integrated fruitfully into the world economy.

Gorbachev is creating what could be called a "normal dictatorship" (i.e., a place where government proceeds against the dissident only legally and only when he organizes). The populist politician Boris Yeltsin has pointed out that Gorbachev's program is one of "half-measures," that his accumulation of power is ominously close to dictatorship, and that he is detached from the populace. (Yeltsin's demagoguery and possible personal problems do not detract from the fact that he correctly sees that Gorbachev's plan for implementing *perestroika* is flawed.)[19]

In May 1989, Gorbachev called for the postponement of local elections and the decentralization of political power with the argument that the country was not yet ready. At best we will see a *Rechtsstaat*, a state that obeys its own laws, some of which will be repressive by U.S. standards. As the "grandfather" of all Sovietologists, George F. Kennan, has put it, the present "freest period Russia has ever known ... does not mean that Russia is becoming like us." It "could not do so."[20] Yet, even if Gorbachev's *perestroika* goes only so far, his effort may well have been significant. He may even have banished fear from Soviet politics. He has put forth a genuine invitation to people to take a hand in guiding the Soviet Union. But *glasnost* has connected Stalinism with the system so closely that Gorbachev, in order to move forward, may have to build a new political system, discarding the Communist party in order to do it. Even his adroitness and daring may not allow this. Yet even his failure would be magnificent. The Crusaders never found the Holy Grail or drove Islam from the Holy Land, but they did change history. Five years of *perestroika* and *glasnost* preclude a return to the "frozen" Soviet Union of Leonid Brezhnev, although what lies beyond a failed *perestroika* and an overheated *glasnost* cannot be imagined. "We cannot preclude the possibility of a drastic turn against the forces of reform in the Soviet Union ..."[21]

So long as progress in a democratic direction continues, Americans will tend to support the "new détente." And it looks as if this progress will continue for a time. But what if it stops? Even then, the United States would continue dealing with the Soviet Union in a routine and formal way, but significant new steps, such as a long overdue strategic arms treaty or a real increase in trade, would become difficult to take. U.S. political culture tends to discourage contacts with those who disappoint us.

U.S. POLICY

Any U.S. policy toward the Soviet Union worthy of the name must be one that improves the relationship, stabilizes international politics, speaks to U.S. and Soviet concerns, both governmental and public in both cases, is acceptable to most of the American people, and is implementable. That is, policy must be both enlightened and realistic. It must make progress toward the reduction of tensions and the solution of problems, while at the same time not moving so fast on the sticky emotional issues that it runs aground on the rocks still existing in our difficult relationship. Both sides will have to do what is so difficult—reach out toward a new relationship while speaking frankly about the present one. The tone of U.S. statements ought to be low key, but our negotiating stance ought to be strong and specific. The Bush administration is trying to learn the trick of it. Maybe it has.

The Malta summit allows some limited forecasts about the near-term. *International context.* The superpowers are less "super," but they are not being replaced by any other power or powers. *Opposing ideologies* are no longer the basis for serious superpower conflict. Both sides want to deal pragmatically with one another and with mutually serious problems. Only here and there in the Third World will ideologies have a disruptive slant. *National power.* Both the United States and the Soviet Union will have to move faster, to scramble, to avert further serious deterioration in their economies. This task, not a new Cold War, will require great effort and energy—and with no firm prospect of success. *Military rivalry.* Modernization and maintenance of significant, though reshaped, forces will continue—but on a much smaller and non-destabilizing scale. (Remember, even during the Great Depression the United States developed and deployed new weapons systems: consider the aircraft carrier and associated planes, the long-range bomber, and the Norden bombsight, not to mention a new rifle. Right now, yet another rifle is being developed to replace the M–16. In the same period the Soviets developed and deployed new tanks, a new rifle,

and other systems.) *Arms control.* Quantum leaps will be taken—
50 percent and greater reductions in strategic arms and massive
cuts and withdrawals in conventional forces will take place. Those
planning a military career has best be both gung ho and geniuses
to boot, and in the U.S. military, they should be prepared to serve
their entire career in the U.S. South, as was the pattern prior to
World War II. *Superpower rivalry in the Third World* will become
mainly a species of diplomatic and economic competition. But the
Soviets will not abandon Cuba or Nicaragua, just reduce aid to them,
and the United States will continue to strive to influence events in
Central America and remain diplomatically involved in southern
Africa. *Trade and technology transfer* will increase as the political
climate warms, but a real increase in U.S.–Soviet trade will require
a qualitatively new Soviet economy and a convertible ruble. The
latter may be produced but the former requires political moves
that Gorbachev seems afraid to take and a cultural transformation
of the Soviet people that will take decades. Poland, Czechoslovakia,
and Hungary may well have capacities for "superchange" that the
"superpower" Soviet Union simply lacks. *Exchanges of people* will
blossom, at least to a point and for a time.

All this requires that U.S. and Soviet politics remain relatively
stable, and that Gorbachev lives and works out an arrangement that
will keep the Soviet peoples, or most of them, both inside the Soviet
Union and waiting peacefully for a better future.

Perhaps, if luck runs, none of the many "land mines" of international politics will blow up for a while, and if any do detonate,
we will wait before we do or say anything until we see how it
actually affects us. No knee-jerk reactions. Possibly we can even
come up with a grand U.S. vision that both matches and meshes
with Gorbachev's. Then, with determination, conviction, and realistic goals, we can gain, along with the Soviets, from the una-
voidably long-term and difficult negotiations that stretch before us.

To get into the mood for this, we might ask ourselves whether
our economic base, our race relations, and our drug situation are
not more serious threats than the Soviet Union. We might also note
that history knows no examples of endless conflict between systems.

NOTES

1. The United States accepted, in effect, the Soviet subjugation of East
Central Europe and, by 1949, was preparing for a massive cut in its armed

forces and military budget when that course was reversed by the Soviet-supported North Korean invasion of South Korea in June 1950. This reversal has stayed in effect until today.

2. Radio Free Europe/Radio Liberty *Soviet/East European Report* 7, no. 2 (October 10, 1989): 2, and *New York Times*, September 21, 1989, p. A15. (Hereafter *NYT*.)

3. *NYT*, September 16, 1989, p. A1. For a recent historically based and statistically sophisticated study on the dangers to peace of multiplicity of states relatively equal in power, a situation to which we are returning, see Manus I. Midlarsky, *The Onset of World War* (Boston: Unwin Hyman, 1988). My review of this book is the May 1990 issue of *The Annals*.

4. For the Soviets, as for many Europeans, the Americans are, or should be, "Westhemispheriki," influential only in the western hemisphere.

5. *NYT*, October 24, 1989, p. A14.

6. *Boston Globe*, October 23, 1989, p. 2 (from *The Washington Post*), and *NYT*, October 11, 1989, p. D2.

7. John le Carré, *The Russia House* (New York: Knopf, 1989), p. 131.

8. "On Gorbachev: A Talk with Andrei Sahkarov," *The New York Review of Books*, December 22, 1988, p. 28.

9. *New York Times*, October 17, 1989, p. A1 and October 19, 1989, p. A7.

10. Alexander Yanov, "Perestroika and Its American Cities," *Slavic Review* 47, no. 4 (Winter 1988–89): 723.

11. RFE/RL, *Soviet East European Report* 7, no. 1 (October 1, 1989): 2.

12. "Rights Policy—or Sham?" *NYT*, January 22, 1989, p. E25.

13. "U.S. Psychiatrists Fault Soviet Units," *NYT*, March 12, 1989, pp. 1, 19.

14. Nicholas Daniloff, "Soviet Standards on Human Rights," *Boston Globe*, January 13, 1989, p. 13.

15. Régis Debray, "When God Fails, Russia Remains," *New Perspective Quarterly* (Winter 1988–89), p. 30, partially reprinted in *Harper's*, April 1989, pp. 22–23.

16. *New York Times*, October 24, 1989, p. A14.

17. *New York Times*, March 20, 1989, p. D4.

18. *Pravda*, March 4, 1989, p. 2.

19. See *Boris Yelstin at Columbia*, Transcript of September 11, 1989 (New York: Harriman Institute, 1989).

20. *NYT*, June 9, 1989, p. A1 and May 3, 1989, p. A1; George F. Kennan, "After the Cold War," *The New York Times Magazine*, February 5, 1989, p. 38.

21. Adam B. Ulam, review of Robert S. McNamara, *Out of the Cold: New Thinking for American Defense-Policy in the 21st Century* (New York: Simon & Schuster, 1989), October 8, 1989, p. 12.

8

Soviet Foreign Policy: A New Era?

Richard F. Staar

The fourth anniversary of the "new era" passed almost unnoticed on March 11, 1989. In the United States, a president's term of office would have been over and a balance sheet of gains/losses drawn up. Not so in the Soviet Union. When Mikhail S. Gorbachev was nominated to an unlimited number of years as general secretary of the Communist Party of the Soviet Union (CPSU), fellow Politburo member Andrei A. Gromyko said of him, "Comrade Gorbachev has a nice smile but iron teeth." The *Gensek* has displayed this congenial smile indeed on television, especially in the West; he has shown his iron teeth by ousting aged leaders like Gromyko, who could have opposed the "new political thinking" in foreign affairs.

FOREIGN POLICY OBJECTIVES

In 1986, less than one year into the "new era," the CPSU's 27th Party Congress adopted a program (previous ones had been announced in 1903, 1919, and 1961) that should have been applicable into the next century. This document is the product of an earlier period, with its traditional slogans, although it does avoid the utopian formulations of the immediately preceding platform under Nikita S. Khrushchev.

The following general foreign policy objectives are spelled out in the most recent CPSU program:

1. cooperation with all member (Communist-Party rules) states of the world socialist system;

2. strengthening relations with (Third World) liberated countries;

3. maintenance of peaceful coexistence and striving for disarmament with capitalist governments;

4. supporting proletarian internationalism within the world worker's and Communist movement.[1]

Since this document is more or less ignored, it would appear that Gorbachev has been attempting to divest himself of certain ideological constraints. We do not know, of course, whether Mrs. Raisa Gorbachev (a former Moscow State University professor on Marxism-Leninism) has any influence on her husband. That ideology certainly does remain important is suggested by an August 24, 1988 note from Gorbachev to the Politburo "On the Question of Reorganizing the Party Apparatus" into six commissions.[2]

One of these is the new ideological commission, chaired by Vadim A. Medvedev, who is a national secretary as well as a member of the 12-man Politburo. The new commission includes 24 other members. The ideology department, under the commission, has six subdivisions. The one dealing with foreign political information and international ties is responsible for "ideological activity in the international arena."[3] It is doubtful whether such an elaborate structure would be created if ideology were no longer important.

On the other hand, by projecting what he calls the "new political thinking," Gorbachev emphasizes a global interdependence that supposedly transcends class parochial interests. Human problems are shared by the whole world. In his speech before the United Nations General Assembly in December 1988, the Soviet leader mentioned the environment more than 20 times and compared ecological destruction with what happens during a war.[4] And then, there is so much talk concerning Leninism.

Lenin supported his interpretation of international events on class interests, held to a world outlook based on a struggle to the death between capitalism and "socialism," and used the term peredyshka (breathing space) to explain his policy of "peaceful coexistence."

Even though they were economically and militarily weak at that time, the Bolsheviks certainly had the courage of their convictions and did not hide behind a facade of maskiroka (deception).

Thus, it would appear that Gorbachev is faced with a choice between Leninism and the "new political thinking." It is impossible to operate in the real world on the basis of (1) an ideology, grounded in the idea of the class struggle, and at the same time on the basis of (2) a theory of global interdependence that supposedly transcends class interests. If the latter is chosen, Marxism will be abandoned in the Soviet Union. However, the Leninist option would make it possible to maintain either a quasi-permanent NEP (New Economic Policy of the 1920's) orientation or a return to a revolutionary type of repression.[5]

Setting ideology aside, it should be noted that Gorbachev's two key foreign policy advisers pragmatically disagreed on which geopolitical areas to emphasize after the 27th Party Congress. Anatoly F. Dobrynin, ambassador to the United States for almost a quarter-century, urged that superpower relations be accorded the highest priority. Alexander N. Yakovlev publicly advised a downgrading of emphasis on the United States and the adoption of a "borderlands" strategy (i.e., concentrating on Western Europe, China, Japan, India, and other areas in close proximity to the Soviet Union). Both approaches were adopted, since there would be no conflict between them in the short run.

One of the two men cited above, Dobrynin, then appeared in the ascendancy, when called back from the United States to become a national secretary and chief of the international department in the central party apparatus. During the restructuring that was announced on September 30, 1988, he lost both positions and only later reappeared as one of the advisers to Gorbachev as Supreme Soviet chairman (government) and not as the party *Gensek*. Dobrynin should be able to provide a different opinion, if asked, from that of the man who may soon emerge as de facto deputy to the Soviet party leader.

Four years younger than Dobrynin, that person is Yakovlev. He has worked in the CPSU as a full-time functionary since age 23. His diplomatic experience is limited to ten years as ambassador to Ottawa. Since returning from this Canadian "exile" in 1983, he has directed the prestigious Institute of the World Economy and International Relations (IMEMO), the CPSU propaganda department, and, over the past three years, successively became a national secretary, Politburo member, and chairman of the new commission on questions of international policy.[6]

Some indication of Yakovlev's view of the United States can be seen from this quotation that appeared in one of his books:

> Reality is such that we must deal with a country [the United States] where freedom is suppressed, where violence flourishes, where trade unions are persecuted, where the press serves Big Business and where the basic rights of the individual are hampered: the right to work, the right to live, the right to get objective information, the right to have materially guaranteed access to true culture and the right to personal security. This is a nation in which militarism and war are the basic means of achieving foreign-policy goals.[7]

The 21 members of Yakovlev's ideological commission include two directors of major research institutes (G. A. Arbatov, United States and Canada; E. M. Primakov, IMEMO), the chief of the armed forces general staff, a vice president of the U.S.S.R. Academy of Sciences (E. P. Velikhov), a first deputy and one deputy foreign minister, the KGB chairman (V. A. Kriushkov), the editor of *Izvestia*, the chief of the international department in the Central Committee apparatus (V. M. Falin), a woman cosmonaut (V. V. Tershkova); an aide to the *Gensek* (A. S. Cherniaiev), but no Dobrynin.[8] It should be noted that many of these individuals have appeared as official spokespersons for the Soviet government in the West.

The most important unit under this commission is the international department under Valentin M. Falin, who succeeded Dobrynin in this position. Responsibilities of the department include relations with the non-ruling Communist and "progressive" parties as well as national liberation movements, international front organizations, friendship societies, clandestine radio stations, and foreign policy related institutes. A separate department deals with bloc relations (i.e., ruling Communist parties).[9] These units represent the working level of the foreign affairs apparatus.

NEW THINKING?

A blueprint for the "new political thinking" was laid out by Gorbachev in his international best-selling book, which has been translated into some 40 foreign languages. He devotes Chapter 3 to a discussion of how he perceives the contemporary world. The basic principle of the new political thinking, according to Gorbachev, is simple: "Nuclear war may not be used as a means for achieving political, economic, ideological or any other objectives."[10]

With reference to Khrushchev's famous statement, "We will bury you" (*my vas zakopaem*), Gorbachev attempts an explanation in terms of the debate among scientists–agronomists during the late 1920s and early 1930s, which supposedly had been called a discussion about "who will bury whom." In any event, Gorbachev assures us in his book that Khrushchev's phrase was improperly understood in the West and that, in any case, it should not be applied to all situations.

He ends this chapter calling for a dialogue with the West as well as for an honest and open foreign policy. Utilizing the channels of public diplomacy, according to Gorbachev, the Soviet Union will strive to make its positions clear to all peoples (i.e., presumably over the heads of their governments). Gorbachev states that the old inertia (by definition, the ideology of the West) is stronger than the new political thinking, although he believes that this situation will change to the advantage of the latter. Indeed, he claims that the future of the world depends on such a transformation.

PROPAGANDA

Assuming that the "new political thinking" will be implemented by exercising power through such "instruments as diplomacy, force [the military], propaganda, and economic rewards or punishments [foreign trade],"[11] how have some of these tools been applied during the recent past? Let us begin with foreign propaganda.

A former director of European and Soviet affairs on the U.S. National Security Council staff has suggested that one of the main objectives of the Soviet propaganda campaign includes both erosion of the belief that Moscow pursues adversarial goals and projection of a world order that blurs East–West distinctions.[12] Gorbachev's address at the United Nations in late 1988, cited in Note 4, represents a masterpiece example of the foregoing. Yakolev's commission on questions of international policy includes supervision over foreign propaganda and, thus, presumably had a hand in drafting the speech.

Parallel with and using the same broadcasting facilities as Radio Moscow is an "unofficial" transmitter, established in 1964, calling itself Radio Peace and Progress (RPP), which can always be disavowed by the Soviet government. During the fall of 1988, RPP claimed that both Iran and Iraq "now realize that imperialist U.S. circles are their common enemy."[13] Unmentioned, of course, was the fact that the Soviet Union supplied weapons to Iraq and the Eastern European regimes did the same for Iran during the war between those two countries. One might add as a footnote that the clandestine "National Voice of Iran" (which had transmitted in Farsi, Kurdish, and Azerbaijani from Baku between 1959 and 1986) has been taken over by RPP with the same radio frequencies and announcers.[14]

During the December 1987 summit meeting in Washington, D.C., Gorbachev promised Charles Z. Wick, then director of the United States Information Agency, that there would be "no more lying" and "no more disinformation." Since that time, however, Soviet government media have made the following false allegations:

- The United States has military advisors in Afghanistan (*TASS*, December 30, 1987)

- The Federal Bureau of Investigation (FBI) assassinated Martin Luther King, Jr. (*Literaturnaia gazeta*, January 20, 1988)

- The 1978 Jonestown massacre in Guyana involved the U.S. government (*Novosti*, December 1988)

- The United States is manufacturing an "ethnic weapon" that kills only non-whites (*Zaria vostoka*, February 19, 1989)

- The Central Intelligence Agency (CIA) assassinated Prime Minister Olof Palme of Sweden, Prime Minister Indira Gandhi of India, and attempted to kill Pope John Paul II (Radio Moscow, February 13, 1988; *TASS*, February 2, 1989)

- The United States manufactured the AIDS virus in a military facility at Fort Detrick, Maryland, and is continuing biological warfare efforts (Radio Moscow, February 13, 1988; *Selskaia zhizn'*, March 3, 1989)

- U.S. citizens purchase Latin American babies to obtain their organs for transplants (*Sovestskaia kultura*, October 25, 1988; (this disinformation was picked up and published in some 50 countries throughout the world)[15]

Despite Gorbachev's public claims to the contrary, disinformation clearly continues to thrive, along with espionage and the theft of high technology,[16] as weapons of the "new political thinking."

MILITARY DOCTRINE

The promise to adopt a "defensive" military doctrine came even earlier than Gorbachev's pledge to abandon disinformation. The political consultative committee of the Warsaw Treaty Organization (WTO) announced this after the May 1987 session in East Berlin, when a separate document on this subject was issued. It pledges not to begin hostilities unless attacked and not to use nuclear weapons first. The document specifically promises that the East will respect the independence and territorial integrity of other states and will not interfere with their internal affairs. Finally, WTO members admit to existing imbalances and asymmetries in certain unspecified armaments and troop categories.[17]

Despite this admission, nothing of consequence really happened during the rest of 1987 of all of calendar year 1988 at the Mutual and Balanced Force Reduction (MBFR) negotiations in Vienna, Austria, which had begun as NATO-WTO talks back in October 1973. Does this mean the East had perpetrated yet another hoax? Reports suggested that the Soviet Union wanted to close down MBFR and establish a new forum that would include all of the countries, including neutrals, situated between the Atlantic Ocean and the Urals. This would happen only if the Conference on Security and Cooperation in Europe follow-on discussions ended to the Soviet Union's satisfaction. However, in the meanwhile, discussions began on a replacement for MBFR.

Gorbachev's speech to the United Nations in December 1988 included an announcement that 500,000 (total circa 5.8 million) Soviet troops would be unilaterally demobilized and 10,000 (total 49,470) tanks withdrawn from the active inventory over the following two years (i.e., 1989 and 1990). This was followed by an article reflecting Soviet defense ministry figures on specific reductions to be carried out also by other pact members.[18] Only one country, Romania, failed to follow the Soviet example, because of a cut in its military budget and armed forces by five percent back in 1986. It is not known at this time what kind of tanks, the obsolescent T–54 (now left behind in Afghanistan) or the latest T–80 model, will be withdrawn.

When then U.S. Secretary of Defense Frank C. Carlucci addressed the Voroshilov Military Academy of the U.S.S.R. Armed Forces in Moscow in August 1988 (some 14 months after the Warsaw Pact document on defensive strategy had been issued), he stated:

First, we have difficulty in reconciling a defensive doctrine with what we see in Soviet force structure and operational strategy as an emphasis on *the offensive*—especially on surprise and maneuver. I refer to such things as the operational maneuver group concept, forward based bridging units, and the heavy emphasis on tanks and artillery. At the same time, we see no shift of emphasis to the kind of forces typically associated with defense.[19]

Secretary Carlucci said that the signs observed from Soviet military exercises were ambiguous and that it would be difficult to differentiate between offensive forces initiating an attack and those prepared to launch a counteroffensive.

Also disturbing were the six tables of figures, released by the Warsaw Pact committee of defense ministers, that allegedly compared the Eastern and Western alliance systems. They differ substantially from data that had been published two months earlier by NATO.[20] The two sets of figures are compared in Table 1. In an interview with TASS, one of the deputy chiefs of a directorate in the Soviet armed forces general staff (Major General Iuri Lebedev) accused the West of excluding figures on naval forces and some of the air forces from its announcement. Subsequently, WTO defense ministers described the NATO data as tendentious and "based on a selective approach."[21] Hardly an auspicious prelude to the negotiations on Conventional Forces in Europe (CFE), which opened March 9, 1989, in Vienna.

What one finds most disconcerting, in the midst of Soviet rhetoric about military budget cuts and conversion of defense industries from production of weapons to consumer goods, are figures on Soviet military production, shown in Table 2. These data indicate that the Soviet Union not only maintained identical production

Table 1
The Balance of Forces in Europe

	WARSAW PACT FORCES		NATO FORCES	
	Warsaw Pact estimate	NATO estimate	Warsaw Pact estimate	NATO estimate
Men under arms	3,573,100*	3,090,000	3,660,200	2,213,593
Tanks	59,470	51,500	30,690	16,424
Armored Personnel Carriers	70,330	71,000	46,900	35,351
Helicopters	2,785**	3,700	5,270	2,419
Combat Aircraft	7,876***	8,250	7,130	3,977

*Includes navy personnel.
**Includes navy helicopters.
***Includes naval aircraft.

Sources: NATO, *Conventional Forces in Europe: The Facts* (Brussels: November 1988), p. 34; *Statement by the Committee of the Ministers of Defense of the Warsaw Treaty Member States* (East Berlin: Panorama DDR, 1989), p. 15.

levels during 1988 as compared with 1986 in most categories of weapons systems, but in many cases, exceeded them.

Uncritical acceptance of the "new political thinking" in the West has led to drastic cuts in military budgets and especially in the procurement of new weapons systems. This has made each new Soviet weapon even more "cost effective" than it would otherwise have been. Hence, it is impossible to avoid the conclusion that the "correlation of forces" is shifting eastward at a faster pace than ever before. A program broadcast over Radio Moscow mentioned the unilateral reduction of 800 aircraft and then listed for 1989 "the MIG–29 and SU–27 fighters, and TU–160 strategic bomber,

Table 2
Soviet Military Production, 1986–88

	1986[1]	1987	1988
Ground Force			
Tanks	3,300	3,500	3,500
Other Armored Fighting Vehicles	3,700	4,050	4,550
Towed Field Artillery	1,100	900	1,100
Self-propelled Field Artillery	900	900	1,100
Multiple Rocket Launchers	500	450	500
Self-propelled AAA	100	100	100
Missiles			
ICBM's	75	125	150
LRINF	25	75	50
SRBM's	600	500	450
SLCM's	1,100	1,100	1,100
SLBM's	100	100	100
Aircraft			
Bombers	50	45	45
Fighters/Fighter-Bombers	650	700	700
Transports	200	175	150
ASW	5	5	5
Military Helicopters	500	450	400
Utility/Trainers	45	10	10
Naval Ships			
Submarines	8	9	9
Surface Warships[2]	9	8	10
Other Surfaced Combatants[3]	60	55	51
Auxiliaries	6	7	7

[1]Some 1986 figures revised to reflect current total production information.
[2]Includes aircraft carriers, cruisers, destroyers, frigates, and corvettes.
[3]Includes patrol combatants, coastal patrol craft, and mine warfare and amphibious warfare ships and crafts.

Source: Central Intelligence Agency and Defense Intelligence Agency, "Gorbachev's Economic Program," *Hearings* (Washington, D.C.: Joint Economic Committee, Congress of the United States 1989), Part 13, pp. 111–12.

and the Russian heavy military transport aircraft" as examples of the new weapons systems.[22]

TRADE AND TECHNOLOGY

The final issue to consider here is the use of trade as an instrument of foreign policy. The late Nikita S. Khrushchev once explained to a group of visiting U.S. senators, "We value trade least for *economic* reasons and most for *political* reasons."[23] Historically, the Soviets have limited or served commercial exchange in order to penalize certain governments. Examples include the total embargo against Yugoslavia (1949), the drastic cutback with China (1965), and the temporary stoppage of oil deliveries to Romania (1980). If this happens with Communist-ruled regimes, the West should be forwarned that it can be done to other countries as well.[24] Two illustrations that come to mind are the attempt to pressure Iceland against joining NATO (1948) and the boycott of Australian wool (1954).

East—West exchange during calendar year 1988 amounted to only 23.5 percent of the Soviet foreign trade total.[25] A decade earlier, at the height of détente, the United States ranked third (after West Germany and Japan) among the best Soviet trading partners, in part due to large U.S. exports of agricultural products. During calendar year 1988, the Soviet target of 194 million tons of grain was 19 percent or 38 million tons short, and the Soviets imported 36 million tons from the United States, Argentina, Australia, and Canada.[26] Although the U.S. share is sizable, with subsidized sales of about 15 million tons to the Soviet Union during 1988, this amount still does not allow the U.S. government to exercise political leverage to any appreciable extent.

In order to finance such large purchases of grain, both the Soviet Union and certain Eastern European states have engaged in "dumping" low-priced items and services in Western Europe. The Federal Republic of Germany has accused Hungary, Poland, and Yugoslavia of offering pharmaceuticals at discounts of almost one-half of production cost. The Soviet merchant marine (Morflot) earns hard currency as a third-flag carrier and has undercut Liner Conference rates by up to 40 percent. As a result, three U.S. shipping companies

(Pacific, Far East, and United States Lines) have been driven out of business.[27]

Despite such unfair practices, the Soviet Union had been able to obtain more than $50 billion worth of high technology from the West during the 1970s. The sale of 164 miniature precision ball-bearing machines facilitated Soviet development of heavy multi-warhead intercontinental ballistic missiles (ICBMs) at a more rapid rate than otherwise would have been possible. Military trucks used in Afghanistan were produced by the supposedly civilian Kama River plant, built with $1.5-billion worth of Western technology. The automated foundry, engines, production line, and computer system all came from the United States. Two large U.S. floating docks are being used to repair Soviet warships at Cam Ranh Bay, Vietnam. In all cases, the United States had received assurances that none of the output from this equipment or technology would be turned over to the Soviet armed forces.[28]

Before the end of 1979, it had become clear that Soviet military capabilities were being improved by legally imported technology from the West. Despite the efforts of CoCom (Coordinating Committee on Multilateral Export Controls), which includes Japan and all NATO member governments except Iceland, there has been considerable leakage of high technology to the East. Soviet countermeasures against CoCom have been directed at circumventing that works through clandestine channels. One of these is KGB Directorate "T" (technology), documentation about which was obtained by the French intelligence service.[29]

In addition, a copy of a secret acquisitions manual, called Das Rote Buch because of its red covers, fell into the hands of the West German government. It has 27 chapters, suggesting the extent of Moscow's high technology "shopping list."[30] Twelve key Soviet defense manufacturing ministries provide the desiderata for specific collection requirements. These are submitted to the Military—Industrial Commission or VPK (Voenno-promyshlennaia Komissiia, which uses the KGB and GRU (Military Intelligence Directorate), civilian and military intelligence, to obtain one-of-a-kind military and dual-use hardware, blueprints, produce samples, and test equipment.[31]

A recent acquisitions operation under this program was frustrated by U.S. Customs Service agents in Miami when they arrested four citizens of the Netherlands. These foreigners were attempting to smuggle a $1.5-million Vax 8800 computer, which had been modified for 50-cycle electric current in the Soviet bloc. Such equipment can be utilized for operation of ballistic missiles and radar installations.[32] The current U.S. Treasury Department list of most wanted high-tech smugglers includes West German, Swiss, British, Austrian, and U.S. citizens.

A second program to obtain modern high technology comes under the Soviet Ministry of Foreign Economic Relations. Microelectronics, computers, communications, machinery, robotics, diagnostic, and other export-controlled equipment are sought to increase the efficiency of Soviet weapon-producing industries. During the 10th Five-Year Plan some 3,500 requirements, submitted by twelve different ministries, were met successfully. However, only one-third of all VPK assignments were fulfilled completely or in part each year, which suggests that Western efforts to prevent illegal high-tech transfer have had some effect.[33]

An example of a significant, if not disastrous, trade diversion publicized in May 1987 involved two prominent Japanese and Norwegian firms. Both of their governments belong to CoCom. Toshiba Machine Company had secretly installed computer-controlled equipment to produce quietly revolving propeller blades for Soviet nuclear submarine sat the Leningrad ship yard. The Kongsberg Vaapenfabrik supplied the software. The contract even included a five-year service obligation.[34] A mere $29 million gave the Soviet Union a military advantage that has complicated submarine tracking for the U.S. navy.

The Foreign Economic Relations Ministry operates from Moscow literally hundreds of trade companies throughout the world. During the early 1980s, some 15 percent of all VPK assignments and 9 percent of the "most critical" ones were satisfied with the help of Ministry officials. They also collected almost one-third of all samples.[35]

The Soviet Union apparently hopes for a direct transfusion of high technology on a massive scale. Western government leaders seem willing, even enthusiastic, about accommodating Gorbachev. During the last three months of 1988, high-ranking officials from Britain, France, the Federal Republic of Germany, Italy, Japan, and others travelled to Moscow with offers of loans that totaled some

$12.2 billion, much in untied credits. The Soviet hard-currency debt by the end of July 1989 had already risen to about $43 billion, the servicing of which absorbs about 60 percent of Soviet export earnings.[36]

In sum, the Soviet agenda with regard to foreign trade is clear: membership in the General Agreement of Tariffs and Trade (GATT), which would facilitate acquisition (on credit at concessionary rates or through Eastern Europe at subsidized rates) of the food, high technology, and hard currency that the Soviet economy cannot produce, and which is essential to provide the population with a minimal diet, the military with advanced weapons, and the Soviet empire with hard cash. The Western agenda is much more nebulous. The only thing clear about it is that taxpayers in the West pay now and hope for developments later over which no one has any control. This may or may not be strictly "Leninism," but it makes sense from the Soviet point of view.

IMPORTANCE OF IDEOLOGY

In conclusion, it seems that ideology—including the practical hybrid called "new thinking"—will continue to play an important role in Soviet foreign policy. Despite the fact that the "socialist commonwealth of nations" has had only 16 party-states as members, the approximately 80 communist parties in other countries have comprised a potent reservoir of support for Moscow, although this may be changing. The so-called national liberation movements throughout the Third World have also been considered allies in the struggle against the "imperialist" camp headed by the United States. So long as Soviet military power "protects" them, Western-supplied cash keeps flowing, and political pressure from Moscow prevents effective aid to their opponents, members of the "world socialist system" will remain as assets.

Gorbachev has sought to reassure the West by announcing a return to the "peaceful coexistence" of the early 1920s under Lenin. It is doubtful, however, that the founder of the Soviet totalitarian state would have continued this policy beyond the peredyshka or respite necessary for economic recovery, even if he had lived after 1924. Lenin was a true believer in Marxism and the ultimate victory of the socialist world, as is Gorbachev today.

The ideological antagonism between capitalism and socialism is manifested in the continuing use of hostile propaganda against the United States. Perhaps the most potentially damaging tactic is the dissemination of forged documents. Prepared by the KGB, they are attributed to U.S. government agencies not only with the intention of discrediting the United States in the eyes of the Third World but also of splitting the NATO alliance. Clandestine radio stations broadcasting false allegations from Eastern Europe and the Soviet Union fulfill the same purpose. Using measures traditionally associated with warfare, the Soviet regime continues to interfere with U.S. foreign policy objectives while publicly proclaiming the end of such hostilities.

A war-fighting and war-survival posture has characterized Soviet military doctrine from its origin. Indeed, deployment of superior strategic offensive forces already has given Moscow the capability of destroying more than 90 percent of all U.S. land-based intercontinental ballistic missiles in their pre-launch configuration. Consequently, the Soviets have little to lose by announcing a less than 10 percent cut over two years in conventional forces. After 15 years and three months of inconclusive MBFR talks at Vienna, does anyone realistically expect the new negotiations on conventional forces in Europe (CFE) to produce significant results? During 1988, the U.S. intelligence community reported that Soviet defense spending had grown by roughly three percent.[37]

One of the Soviet Union's weak points, however, is the need for trade, credits, and advanced technology from the West, especially the United States. To gain access to world markets and receive acceptance as a reliable partner in international business transactions, the Soviet Union hopes to offer the "carrot" of good behavior to countries reluctant to welcome it into the global business community. The desire of U.S. allies to tap into Soviet natural resources and a starved domestic market may well exacerbate tensions in NATO and in U.S.–Japanese relations. In this way, the Soviet Union threatens both the political as well as the economic stability of the West.

THE AMERICAN STANCE

What, then, can the United States do, if it wants to maintain "normal" relations with the Soviet Union and at the same time protect itself from whatever ultimate fate Moscow might have in store for us? We can learn from the regime in Beijing, which long ago set out three preconditions for normalizing government-to-government relations with the other Communist superpower: (1) a substantial reduction in the estimated two million Soviet troops deployed along Chinese borders, (2) withdrawal of all Soviet armed forces from Afghanistan, and (3) evacuation of Vietnamese troops from Cambodia. The Chinese held out for almost 30 years, and Gorbachev arrived in Beijing for a summit meeting in mid-May 1989. Of course, there is no question of Chinese aid to the Soviet Union.

Unfortunately, the United States does not have that kind of illusion-free statesmanship. Secretary of State James Baker could make it clear to his counterpart the next time they meet that the United States will no longer tolerate the continuing active measures campaign, violations of arms control treaties, intensification of espionage, the massive $1 billion per year economic and military assistance to Nicaragua, and the same tactics at the CFE talks that had stymied MBFR. A warning that negotiations on a treaty for strategic arms reductions will remain on hold, until the Soviet Union begins to act like a civilized member of the world community, might bring surprising results.

But such words would have to be backed up by resolve to maintain U.S. armed forces capable of fighting the Soviet Union if necessary, resolve to cut off Western subsidies through secondary boycotts, and most of all, resolve to call the Soviet colonial empire by its rightful name.

A final suggestion is that the U.S. government take some lessons from the Chinese: see the "new political thinking" for what it really is, make clear our position on negotiable points and situations, and let the Soviets (eager to accommodate the West in the hope of rescuing their economy) make truly conciliatory moves before we decide to change our stance, and certainly before we decide to support Gorbachev's "new era."

NOTES

1. *Programma KPSS: novaia redaktsiia* (Moscow: Politizdat, 1988), pp. 60–74, elaborates on these points.

2. Interview with A. S. Kapto, chief of the ideology department, in *Pravda*, February 20, 1989, p. 2.

3. Membership on all six commissions received Central Committee approval and appeared in *Pravda*, November 29, 1988, pp. 1–2.

4. M. S. Gorbachev's speech at the UNGA was published in full in *Vestnik Ministerstva Inostrannykh Del SSSR*, no. 24 (December 31, 1988), pp. 1–8.

5. I owe this formulation to Professor R. Judson Mitchell, especially in Chapter 10 of his manuscript entitled "Soviet Political Leadership from Brezhnev to Khrushchev," to be published by Hoover Institution Press in early 1990.

6. Alexander G. Rahr, comp., *A Biographic Directory of 100 Leading Soviet Officials*, 4th ed. (Munich: Radio Free Europe/Radio Liberty, 1988), pp. 223–25.

7. Alexander N. Yakovlev, *Ot Triumena do Reigana* (Moscow: Molodaia gvardiia, 1984), p. 339; translated under the title *On the Edge of an Abyss* (Moscow: Progress Publishers, 1985), p. 400.

8. See Note 3 above and Central Intelligence Agency, *Directory of Soviet Officials: National Organizations* (Washington, D.C.: Directorate of Intelligence, 1989), LDA 89–10149, p. 107.

9. Chart, "Moscow's Evolving Active Measures Apparatus," *Disinformation*, no. 11 (Winter 1989): 10–12.

10. M. S. Gorbachev, *Perestroika i novoe myshlenie* (Moscow: Politizdat, 1987), p. 143.

11. Philip G. Roeder, *Soviet Political Dynamics* (New York: Harper & Row, 1988), p. 407.

12. John Lenczowski, "Soviet Propaganda and Active Measures: 1988," *Disinformation*, no. 8 (Winter 1988): 10.

13. Cited by U.S. Information Agency, Office of Research, *Soviet Propaganda Trends*, no. 41 (October 27, 1988): 6.

14. *The Economist Foreign Report* no. 1948 (December 11, 1986), London.

15. U.S. Information Agency, "Soviet Active Measures in an Age of Glasnost" in *Report to Congress* (Washington, D.C.: Office of Research, March 1988), pp. 2–3, 7.

16. Richard F. Staar, "The High Tech Transfer Offensive of the Soviet Union," *Strategic Review* 17, no. 2 (Spring 1989): 32–39.

17. John J. Karch, "Warsaw Treaty Organization," in Richard F. Staar, ed., *1988 Yearbook on International Communist Affairs* (Stanford, Ca.: Hoover Institution Press, 1988), pp. 375–76. For the document itself, see "Concerning Military Doctrine," *Krasnaia zvezda*, May 30, 1987, p. 1.

18. *Argumenty i fakty*, no. 6 (February 11–17, 1989): 8.

19. The Honorable Frank C. Carlucci, Secretary of Defense, "Prospects for the U.S.–Soviet Dialogue," *Press Release*, no. 381–88 (August 1, 1988), p. 3. Emphasis in original.

20. NATO, *Conventional Forces in Europe: The Facts* (Brussels: Information Service, 1988), p. 34; *Pravda*, January 30, 1989, p. 5.

21. Cited by Michael Dobbs, "Warsaw Pact Sees Parity with West," *Washington Post*, January 31, 1989, p. 21.

22. TASS over Radio Moscow, Foreign Broadcast Information Service (FBIS), Daily Report, Soviet Union, August 16, 1989, p. 1.

23. Quoted in the *New York Times*, September 16, 1955, p. 48. Emphasis added.

24. Richard F. Staar, *USSR Foreign Policies after Détente*, rev. ed. (Stanford, Ca.: Hoover Institution Press, 1987), pp. 132)–33.

25. *Vneshniaia torgovlia*, no. 3 (March 1989; insert.

26. TASS report from Moscow (January 21, 1989), published in the *New York Times* on the following day.

27. Curtis Cate, ed., *The Challenge of Soviet Shipping* (New York: National Strategy Information Center, Inc., 1984), pp. 6–9.

28. *Soviet Acquisition of Militarily Significant Western Technology* (Washington, D.C.: Department of Defense, September 1985), p. 3; Ambassador Alan Wendt, "U.S. Export Control Policy: Its Present and Future Course," *Current Policy*, Washington, D.C.: Department of State, June 14, 1988, no. 1094.

29. Thierry Wolton, *Le KGB en France* (Paris: Grasset, 1986), p. 312; Philip Hanson, "Soviet Industiral Espionage," *RIIA Discussion Papers* (London: Royal Institute of International Affairs, 1987), p. 39.

30. Bundesministerium des Innern, *Das "Rote Buch" oder wie die UdSSR westliche Technologien beschafft* (Bonn: 1985), p. 4.

31. *Soviet Acquisition*, p. 6.

32. George Volsky, "Computer Suspect Called Part of Ring," *New York Times*, December 24, 1988, p. 6.

33. *Soviet Acquisition*, p. 25–28.

34. *Wall Street Journal*, April 25, 1988, p. 22.

35. *Soviet Acquisition*, pp. 20–21.

36. Peter Passel, "Western Credit for Moscow?" *New York Times*, July 31, 1989, pp. A–1, C–9.

37. Central Intelligence Agency and Defense Intelligence Agency, "The Soviet Economy in 1988 (Paper presented to the Joint Economic Committee of the U.S. Congress, Washington, D.C., April 14, 1989).

9

New Soviet Thinking on Conflict and Cooperation in the Third World

Robert K. German

The outside world continues to be amazed, but generally pleased, with what we have seen transpiring inside the Soviet Union. The dramatic changes make it even more urgent now to evaluate old myths in the light of today's new realities than it was 26 years ago, when Senator Fulbright first challenged us to do so. What we take to be today's realities make those of 1964 pale by comparison. And while we are impressed with the efforts at internal reform of the Soviet economy and Soviet society, what is of greater importance for us in the West is the apparent change in Moscow's attitude toward international relations. We seem to be seeing a more responsible, less aggressive Soviet Union, and we are told that this changing conduct is a result of "new thinking"—a new way of looking at the world and the Soviet Union's place in it.

To help evaluate this new Soviet thinking—to judge whether it represents a new reality or is simply the creation of a new myth—we might usefully take a closer look at old thinking and how that affected the relationship between the United States and the Soviet Union. I will concentrate on the role of the United States and the Soviet Union in the Third World and their attitudes toward regional conflicts. At first glance, this topic may seem peripheral to some of the major issues between our two countries, particularly the nuclear balance and the urgent need to lower the level of military confrontation. Yet, in truth, developments in the Third World are very much a critical part of the U.S.—Soviet relationship. After all, there are few who seriously fear that the Soviets will launch a nuclear attack on the United States, and probably none who expect a U.S. attack on the Soviet Union. That does not mean, however, that the danger of nuclear war has evaporated—most people would agree that the most plausible scenario for a nuclear war (leaving aside the possibility of a computer malfunction) involves escalation of a local conflict in some region of the world in which both the United States and the Soviet Union have a significant stake.

Let me go back a bit to reflect on the atmosphere that prevailed when Senator Fulbright first spoke of "old myths and new realities." I remember well what I think was the Senator's first visit to the Soviet Union, when he led a delegation of distinguished senators to Moscow to accompany Secretary of State Dean Rusk at the signing of the Limited Test Ban Treaty. I was one of the U.S. Embassy officers privileged to sit in on the meeting Senator Fulbright and his Senate colleagues had with counterparts from the Supreme Soviet—the first such meeting in history.

Certainly those were historic days. The signing of the Test Ban Treaty in August 1963, only nine months after we had teetered on the brink of nuclear disaster, was greeted with a great sense of relief—and not just by those of us who had weathered the Cuban missile crisis in Moscow. The entire world saw the treaty—the first significant post-war arms control agreement—as a sign that sanity was, at last, about to prevail.

That development was no doubt one of the "new realities" Senator Fulbright had in mind when he delivered his lecture on "Old Myths and New Realities" the following spring. And yet, for a variety of reasons, that promising first step did not, after all, lead to an uninterrupted march toward peace. Developments behind the scenes often continued to run counter to the more encouraging surface appearances.

In reviewing Senator Fulbright's 1964 lecture, I was particularly struck by one passage. In assessing the world scene at that time Senator Fulbright stated that:

the character of the Cold War has, for the present at least, been profoundly altered: by the drawing back of the Soviet Union from extremely aggressive policies; by the implicit repudiation, by both sides, of a policy of "total victory"; and by the establishment of an American strategic superiority which the Soviet Union appears to have tacitly accepted because it has been accompanied by assurances that it will be exercised by the United States with responsibility and restraint.[1]

We know that exactly the opposite was the case. Humiliated and infuriated by having to back down when the confrontation came in the Caribbean, the Soviets swore they would never permit that to happen again. Far from accepting U.S. superiority, they embarked on a relentless military buildup that has continued until quite recently—and may even be continuing today.

I mention this not to suggest that Senator Fulbright should have been better able than anyone else to pierce the veil of Kremlin secrecy in 1964. Certainly, he was more foresighted and more courageous than most of his contemporaries in pointing out the fundamental changes that were occurring on the world scene. My point, simply, is that it was the Soviet military buildup spurred by the Cuban missile crisis, and particularly the decision to build a blue-water navy, that transformed the Soviet Union—historically a continental power—into a global power. The resultant capability to project Soviet power worldwide has meant that the interaction of U.S. and Soviet interests is no longer limited to the Eurasian land mass, but can and does occur in unlikely spots all around the globe. It is primarily thanks to that development that local conflicts have taken on so important a role in U.S.–Soviet relations.

Fate also intervened to bring a temporary halt to the improvement in relations that had seemed so promising at the time of the signing of the Test Ban Treaty. The two statesmen most responsible for the treaty soon left the scene. The tragic assassination of President Kennedy came less than four months later, and Khrushchev himself was unceremoniously ousted from office by his colleagues the following year.

Events in other parts of the world also served to reactivate the Cold War. The deepening U.S. involvement in Vietnam played a role, and the June 1967 Middle East War raised East–West tensions to new levels. Perhaps most significant was the Soviet invasion of

Czechoslovakia in 1968, which brought a halt to plans for President Lyndon Johnson to visit the Soviet Union and initiate talks on strategic arms limitations.

The early 1970s saw another thaw in relations that again seemed to herald an end to the Cold War, but that period of détente, like earlier periods of lessened tension, proved remarkably short-lived.

Today, however, we feel even more confident than before that the Cold War is finally coming to an end. Some, in fact, even proclaim that it is over. Yet no one would deny that serious issues remain between the Soviet Union and the United States.

We may, on occasion, have been distressed by the tendency of a U.S. president to reduce serious issues to aphorisms and anecdotes, but we have to admit that Ronald Reagan had a knack for expressing truths in everyday terms. One of his frequently stated and most quotable propositions was that "nations don't distrust each other because they're armed—they're armed because they distrust each other."

REGIONAL ISSUES

It was in the spirit of that truth that President Reagan maintained, when the path to the summit finally opened up, that his conversations with General Secretary Gorbachev were not going to be limited to weapons and arms control. Rather, they also had to deal with the root causes of the distrust between the two countries. And it was for that reason that the president insisted on the now well–known four-point agenda—arms control, to be sure, but also human rights, bilateral relations (in particular, expanding human contacts and improving cultural, scientific, and educational ties), and—the fourth item on the agenda—regional issues.

It was the lesson of the SALT II Treaty, among other things, that motivated the president to insist on a discussion of all of these issues. By 1979, the United States had become disillusioned with détente. Our relations were so strained that whatever inherent flaws there may have been in the SALT II Treaty, the treaty was in deep trouble before it was signed and sent to the Senate in the summer of 1979. And it was the Soviet invasion of Afghanistan at the end of 1979 that sounded the death knell for the treaty.

The Soviet general secretary, on the other hand, initially resisted the U.S. effort to discuss what he treated as extraneous issues. Because he considered the nuclear danger the major problem facing our two nations, Gorbachev at first insisted that efforts to control the nuclear arms race should be the only subject worthy of conversation at the summit level. In fact, when he finally accepted President Reagan's invitation for a meeting in 1985, it seemed clear his only objective was to try to kill the Strategic Defense Initiative.

As time went on, however, Gorbachev himself began to accept the reality that any new successes in the field of arms control would not be accepted by the American people or the U.S. senate, if there were no improvements in other areas of our relationship. Indeed, by the third and fourth Reagan–Gorbachev summits, the Soviets—perhaps making a virtue of necessity, perhaps because they had been truly converted—seemed to enter enthusiastically into discussion of these other items on the agenda.

It is really hard to say which was more difficult initially for Gorbachev to accept as a topic for discussion—human rights or regional issues. For many years the Soviets had branded any attempt to discuss the human rights situation in the Soviet Union as interference in their internal affairs. We know that Gorbachev himself bristled the first few times the subject was raised with him. Yet a transformation began to occur as the Soviets began to realize that this attitude was counterproductive. In fact, they began to take the offensive, not only expressing willingness to listen to what we had to say about the way the Soviet regime treated its citizens, but also beginning to demand answers to questions about what we planned to do about what they called U.S. human rights problems, such as crime in the streets, poverty, and homelessness.

Gorbachev was obviously taxing the credibility of the world when he claimed, from the rostrum of the United Nations General Assembly in December 1988, that, "There are no people in places of imprisonment in the Soviet Union who have been sentenced for their political or religious convictions."[2] Yet it is true that, in recent years, the Soviets have made welcome progress in the human rights field. Most of the more prominent political prisoners have been released, many of the divided-family cases have been resolved, and there has been a marked increase in emigration.

The changing Soviet attitude toward regional disputes is no less encouraging. In the late 1970s and early 1980s, the Soviets simply did not believe us when we told them their conduct in the Third World was deeply disturbing and had a very negative effect on the state of our bilateral relations, that it affected issues like ratification of the SALT II Treaty. I think it really was impossible for them to believe that a Democratic president could not get a Democratic senate to consent to ratification of a treaty that he wanted to see brought into force. Rather, they tended to believe that, somehow, the sinister influence of an anti-Soviet Zbigniew Brzezinski had caused President Carter to abandon his support for the SALT II Treaty.

As a result, our effort to discuss regional issues with Soviet officials were for many years unsuccessful. When we brought up the subject of Afghanistan, they maintained that the fraternal assistance they provided to a neighboring friend was no one else's business. The Soviet-supported Vietnamese occupation of Cambodia, they said, was something we should discuss with the Vietnamese if it troubled us. Similarly, if we were bothered by the presence of Cuban troops in Angola and Ethiopia, that was something to discuss with Havana, not Moscow. And when we raised questions about Soviet military aid to Nicaragua, the general response was to deny that such aid was being provided.

CHANGING ATTITUDES

In the last few years, we have seen striking changes in the Soviet attitude on many of these issues. Most remarkable of all, of course, has been the withdrawal of Soviet forces from Afghanistan—and not only the withdrawal, but the fact that once the Soviets had made the decision to cut their losses and bring the troops home, they welcomed the participation of the United States as a joint guarantor of the 1988 Geneva agreements.

There are indications that the Soviets played a constructive role in persuading the Vietnamese to announce their intention to withdraw from Cambodia. By all accounts, the Soviet role in the negotiations leading to the agreement on Angola and Namibia, including the withdrawal of Cuban troops, was also constructive. There have even been reports that the Soviets are becoming disillusioned with the Mengistu regime in Ethiopia and may be putting pressure on it to try to bring an end to the debilitating civil war.

Each of these situations is different, of course, and each can be explained by the facts of the particular situation. The open question is whether these developments reflect only a temporary Soviet disentanglement from some of the more troublesome Third World conflicts that have proven counterproductive to Soviet interests, or whether, on the other hand, they reflect a fundamental change in the Soviet approach to international relations.

Obviously, only time will tell. And while we say, quite rightly, that deeds speak louder than words, in this case the deeds, while encouraging, are ambiguous, and it is interesting to look at the words as well. Because the Soviet regime bases its legitimacy on its ideology, shifts in conduct have to be justified by shifting interpretations of those ideological underpinnings. What emerges from leadership speeches and theoretical writings is that "new thinking" has not been uniformly accepted in the Soviet Union. There are ongoing behind-the-scenes debates on many issues, including the question of relations with the Third World.

PEACEFUL COEXISTENCE

The way some of the buzzwords like "class struggle" and "peaceful coexistence" are being used may seem obscure, but for the ideological purist they have serious connotations as well as operational significance. It is important to recall that the Marxist-Leninist view of history, based on dialectical materialism and historical determinism, is that the driving force of history is a struggle between classes. It was the class struggle that led to the evolution from slave-holding to feudal to capitalist to socialist societies. Once the Soviet Union proclaimed itself a socialist state, its theorists saw the possibility of conflict between states as a future form of class struggle.

Many of our attitudes in the West today are still influenced by Stalin's assertions that war between the capitalist world and the socialist world was inevitable. We tend to downplay the significance of the Khrushchev's rediscovery—out of an appreciation of the dangers of nuclear war—of the fact that Lenin had actually denied the inevitability of war and, if fact, had called for peaceful coexistence between the capitalist and socialist states.

But peaceful coexistence, as Khrushchev and his successors used the term, had a special meaning. They defined it as a continuation of the class struggle by all means short of war. Given this well-known Soviet interpretation, it was somewhat surprising that President Nixon, at his first meeting with General Secretary Brezhnev, accepted the concept of peaceful coexistence. In the Declaration on Basic Principles of Relations between the United States and the Soviet Union—the so-called "code of conduct"—signed at the 1972 summit, Nixon and Brezhnev agreed that the United States and Soviet Union, "would proceed from the common determination that, in the nuclear age, there is no alternative to conducting their mutual relations on the basis of peaceful coexistence."[3]

Nixon and Kissinger—as we know, for example, from the detailed account in the excellent book *Détente and Confrontation* by Raymond Garthoff—attached very little significance to the Basic Principles declaration. The Soviets, on the other hand, considered it a great victory. They hailed it as having almost the status of a treaty, of greater significance than the SALT I agreement that was signed on the same occasion.

The Soviets had made no secret of their interpretation of peaceful coexistence. Indeed, spokesmen from Brezhnev on down had insisted loudly that peaceful coexistence among states did not mean an end to the class struggle or support for national liberation movements. On the contrary, it was frequently asserted that peaceful coexistence and détente would aid national liberation and the progressive and socialist revolutionary class struggle. The 1977 Soviet Constitution—the so-called Brezhnev Constitution—which stated that the foreign policy of the Soviet Union would be based on peaceful coexistence of states with different social systems, also listed as one of the objectives of Soviet foreign policy the support of the struggle of people for national liberation and social progress.

DISENGAGEMENT?

It is this background that makes the Soviet debate over new thinking and the proper relationship to Third World liberation and revolutionary movements more meaningful. It is worth nothing, however, that this debate did not originate in the Gorbachev era; the trend toward reexamination of Third World entanglements was apparent much earlier. Theoretical writings after the 25th Party

Congress in 1981 made it clear that there was a behind-the-scenes battle at that time over this issue and over the dedication to the theory of class struggle. There were other signs before the end of the Brezhnev era of Soviet disillusionment with excessive involvement in Third World trouble spots.

Nevertheless, it is Gorbachev who has had the courage (and the backing) to make some moves toward what appears to be disengagement. One indication that Gorbachev's actions have been troubling not only to conservative Soviet ideologues but also to Moscow's more revolutionary clients came at the time of the celebration of the 70th anniversary of the 1917 Bolshevik Revolutionary, and other left-wing groups to a meeting during the celebrations in Moscow. Most came, but one who was conspicuous by his late arrival was Fidel Castro, who thereby managed to avoid listening to Gorbachev's opening speech on November 2—a move that was widely interpreted as a show of Castro's displeasure over the new thinking and, with it, implied support of revolutionary movements. Castro was on hand for later speeches and the closing ceremonies, but he was clearly disappointed that Gorbachev did not use this significant occasion—the celebration of the Bolshevik Revolution and its impact on the course of world history—to reaffirm what had been the ritualistic Soviet support for national liberation movements. What he had to say about class struggle was equally disturbing.

In a speech on November 4 to a meeting of representatives of the 178 parties and movements who were attending the festivities, Gorbachev spoke of "new aspects of the content of the idea of peaceful coexistence," saying that these demanded from political movements a "new analysis and reinterpretation of their tasks, the overcoming of the ideological schemes and stereotypes." On that occasion, Gorbachev also asserted that it was "no longer possible to view world development merely from the viewpoint of the struggle between two opposing social systems." And he went on to say that "both class interests and general human interests are, so to speak, fused into one."[4]

"HUMAN VALUES"

In June 1988, at the extraordinary 19th Party Conference in Moscow, Gorbachev again highlighted this concept of "general human values," attributing it to Marx and Lenin, who he said had dialectically united general human values with social and class values. Less than a month later, Foreign Minister Eduard Shevardnadze discussed the significance of the 19th Party Congress in a conference at the Soviet Foreign Ministry. In the relevant passages of his speech published in *Pravda* on July 26, 1988, Shevardnadze also referred to common human values, saying that this concept gave "the philosophy of peaceful coexistence . . . a different content." And he added that, "we refuse to see in [peaceful coexistence] a specific form of class struggle."

What makes these seemingly esoteric formulations more interesting is the speech that Igor Ligachev, Gorbachev's most powerful conservative critic, made in Gorky three weeks later, on August 5, 1988. The full text of that speech was not published, but the August 6 edition of *Pravda* reported that it "touched on questions of CPSU foreign policy, in particular on the correlation between general human and proletarian-class interests." Then, in what appears to be a quote from Ligachev's speech, *Pravda* went on to say, "We proceed from the class nature of international relations. Any other formulation of the issue only introduces confusion into the thinking of Soviet people and our friends abroad. Active involvement in the solution of general human problems by no means signifies any artificial 'braking' of the social and national liberation struggle. And M. S. Gorbachev's report at the 19th Party Conference reaffirmed the CPSU's solidarity with the working people of the entire world."

Ligachev's was not the last work, however, for Gorbachev reasserted the "supremacy" of the common human idea in his December 1988 speech at the United Nations General Assembly.

What seems to emerge from all of this is that not everyone in the leadership has accepted this downplaying of the class-struggle view of history. Nevertheless, Gorbachev has laid the ideological framework for at least a temporary retrenchment from some parts of the Third World and for a less adventuresome approach to regional conflicts. Even so, his emphasis on interdependence, on an integral world, on "common human values" is insufficient to tell us what the Soviet approach is likely to be to any specific situation in the future. Indeed, what we see as a constructive role in some areas—particularly Afghanistan, but also Cambodia, Angola, and possibly Ethiopia—has by no means been replicated everywhere—for example, in Nicaragua and Central America.

AMBIGUOUS ACTIVISM

Soviet aid to Nicaragua appears to be continuing at about the same rate as it has been for the last three or four year—that is, military aid of between $500 and $550 million a year and economic aid of something over $300 million a year. Soviet officials, including their ambassadors in Washington and Managua, have occasionally suggested that Moscow would like to reduce this assistance. Nevertheless, at a 1989 meeting in Vienna between Secretary of State Baker and Foreign Minister Shevardnadze, the Soviets apparently maintained the position that they would halt their aid to the Sandinistas only if the United States agrees to terminate its aid to all of the countries in Central America—obviously a nonstarter.

There is also a mischief-making potential in the Soviet offer to give up its newly acquired military bases in Vietnam if the United States will evacuate its bases in the Philippines.

Moscow's role in efforts to bring the bloody Iran–Iraq war to an end was an ambiguous one. Although the Soviets cooperated in the adoption of U.N. Security Council Resolution 598 in 1987, calling for a cease fire, they played what the U.S. administration considered a less-than-helpful role in refusing to agree to put teeth into 598 or a follow-on resolution. It was obviously their longer-range interest in reestablishing a favorable position in Iran at some future date that led to an unwillingness to agree to sanctions on Iran for refusal to comply with the cease-fire resolution, thus arguably prolonging the settlement process.

Foreign Minister Shevardnadze's trip through the Middle East in 1989 indicated that the Soviets are once more attempting to play an active role in the Middle East peace process. This influence is likely to remain limited, however, so long as they refuse to establish diplomatic relations with Israel.

CONCLUSIONS

There are several conclusions that I would draw from all of this:

—First, the Soviets will probably continue to cut back on their commitments in areas where Soviet interests are marginal, such as Angola and Mozambique.

—Second, in the future they will be much more cautious to look before they leap—that is, they will be less precipitate about providing assistance to the Third World regime or revolutionary movement without more carefully calculating costs and benefits.

—But, third, they will not abandon any of their principal clients in the Third World, particularly Cuba and Vietnam, and they will continue to make available arms and other assistance to key Third World countries such as Syria and Libya.

—Fourth, they will undoubtedly continue the trend of improving relations with major developing countries such as India, Mexico, and Brazil, and they will overcome their ideological aversion to developing economic ties with countries like South Korea.

—And finally, as in the past, they will be prepared to take advantage of new opportunities that may arise when they consider the strategic benefits to be high enough. Neither the economic cost, for example, nor the impact on relations with the United States, it seems to me, would deter the Soviet Union from taking advantage of a hypothetical situation in which a new regime in Iran continued to display hostility toward the United States but began to make friendly overtures toward the Soviet Union.

REALITIES AND MYTHS

Where does all this leave us in the world between myth and reality? The old myth that I think we have to work hard to dispel is "world domination." Probably no Soviet leader since Stalin has actually believed that conquering the world is possible or even desirable. (I suspect, however, that Gorbachev is convinced that the course of history is moving in Moscow's favor, even though he refrains from saying so.)

At the same time, we have to be cautious about accepting too readily what appears to be developing as a new myth, which might be called "world cooperations"—that is, that thanks to the new thinking about global interdependence, we need no longer worry about Soviet assertiveness or expansionist tendencies. Promises to reduce Soviet military forces to a level of reasonable sufficiency and to convert to a purely defensive military posture are welcome indeed. But until we see these promises converted into reality, it is too soon to let down our guard.

Meanwhile, Soviet and U.S. interests will continue to overlap in many parts of the world. It seems unavoidable that the relationship will often be a competitive one. Yet, with sensible leadership on both sides, it need not be confrontational. Indeed, in many instances it can be a cooperative one. The United States should emulate the new–found Soviet enthusiasm for a more active role for the United Nations in international peacekeeping efforts. We should also engage actively in international efforts to resolve some of the ecological and health problems that transcend national boundaries.

Recent trends are encouraging. If they continue, we may be able to say that a more responsible approach to regional problems is not just a myth but one of the new realities.

NOTES

1, J. W. Fulbright, *Old Myths and New Realities* (New York: Random House, 1964), p. 5.

2. Excerpts from Mikhail S. Gorbachev's speech to the United Nations General Assembly, *New York Times*, December 8, 1988.

3. Declaration of Basic Principles of Relations (1972), printed in *SALT II Treaty: Background Documents*, Committee on Foreign Relations, U.S. Senate November 1979 (Washington: U.S. Government Printing Office), pp. 55–58.

4. *Pravda*, November 5, 1988.

10

Europe and the Superpowers: A Conservative View

Enno von Loewenstern

Twenty years ago the question was raised as to why 200 million Americans had to defend 300 million Europeans. The figures have change upward, but the problem has been the same. There is also the question of why the Europeans always have to make trouble, sometimes feeling overdefended and sometimes feeling left in the lurch. Part of the answer may be found in the geostrategic aspect of the continent between the superpowers. This means, necessarily, the military aspect. Where lies the military threat to Western Europe? Who is likely to attack whom? This is not a pleasant question to ask today, what with détente and general hope that this new miracle man Mikhail Gorbachev will set everything right. But when you talk disarmament you have to proceed from an existing threat. If there is no threat, you do not have to set up conferences about disarmament; you disarm unilaterally, because no state and no government that does not wish to threaten—which is incompatible with democracy anyway—and that does not feel threatened, will keep arms just for the sake of spending money.

So, then, who threatens Western Europe? Obviously not the Western superpower. The threat has come from the superpower that declared world revolution and proletarian internationalism its bound duty, that has had an aggressive military doctrine, that kept 400 million people in bondage, and that, while often protesting its allegedly peaceful intentions, has never yet managed to explain why it would, for instance oppress East Germans for the sake of historical materialism but would not reach out and oppress West Germans for the same cause, if only the guard were let down.

GEOSTRATEGIC PROBLEM

Here lies the geostrategic problem—not so much in matters of defense, for 400 million people in highly developed countries, even if often rather parochial and quarrelsome, are nevertheless better on your side than on the other side. The problem begins with disarmament. For as long as peace on earth cannot be achieved by simply establishing good will toward all men, you may use arms reduction as a surrogate. Here the recipe seems simple to some: let us achieve equal strength and there will be no threat left, for all strategists from Sun Zi to Clausewitz have shown that the defense is superior to the attack and that the aggressor therefore needs a numerical superiority for at least four to one—which, incidentally, has equalled the Warsaw Pact superiority in Europe.

Now Gorbachev himself has admitted an "asymmetry" to exist. The answer, then, seems to be this: let him scale down his superiority to symmetry, and the threat will be removed; from there we may proceed to ever lower numbers. Now, it may be doubtful whether mere symmetry is a guarantee of nonaggression, for when Hitler attacked France in May 1940, his army was not superior, it was not even equal in strength instead, it had far fewer tanks than the French—about half their number, not even considering the British Expeditionary Force. And yet Hitler was successful. But let us not dwell on that; of course symmetry would be tremendous progress from present-day Eastern superiority. But here the problem begins.

If there were no Western Europe, or if it were sort of geographically tucked in the U.S. underbelly, there would not be much of a problem in principle. Americans and Soviets would simply count men, tanks, planes, and missiles. All you would have to do then is to agree on present and future numbers and to make sure that nobody cheats. But Western Europe is there, and very much exposed. And the easternmost country of Western Europe—speaking strategically, not in a strict geographical sense—is the Federal Republic of Germany, vulgo West Germany.

An attack would strike West Germany, not Western Europe. That must clearly be seen. Despite all the talk about ever-closer Common Market relations, Europe is still not a federal state, but a "Europe of Nations," as Charles de Gaulle put it. And it will not be a United Nations of Europe in any foreseeable time, if ever; the language barrier will prohibit that. We will have German reunification and the collapse of the communist threat and God knows what changes before the day can be foreseen when the French or the British will yield national sovereignty to a government not run by a majority of British or French—not to mention Spaniards or Germans.

The Europeans made the most terrible mistake of their history, since breaking up the Frankish empire in 843, in abolishing their common language, Latin, in favor of tribal languages. Thus, Europe is not one state but an alliance. If an attack struck the state of Arkansas there would be no doubt from San Diego up to Maine that the United States of America had been attacked and must rally to the defense. If an attack struck West Germany we have the assurance that our allies will help us. But this help will always be governed by the several national interests. It may be held that the national interest of every Western European country requires unstinting help to every ally in distress. But we cannot be assured that the statesmen in charge will always see it so. That is what makes every alliance precarious by definition.

If the worst happens, will the French, for instance, regard us like unto brethren or like unto a glacis? That question has never been answered in detail. The French may mean well; they may hold back only for reasons of raison, of national principle, but that is speculation, not assurance. It is very well to advise the Germans not to be hysterical. But strategy today is not a question of counting heads and strengths and figuring whether we can win another battle on the Catalonian plains; strategy today means deterring any attack, any war with its destruction even of the "victorious" side or at least the German-speaking part of it.

MISSILE REMOVAL AND NEGOTIATIONS

For 40 years the Germans withstood the pressures of political forces who told them that they were the stupid glacis; that the French would never "mourir pour Bonn," nor would the Americans. But now disarmament creates a new situation. Ironically, its very first step, the INF (intermediate-range nuclear forces) treaty, which led to the removal of intermediate-range missiles (Pershing II and cruise missiles from Germany, SS–20 from the Soviet side) has seriously weakened Western defense and, thus, deterrence.

There has been two primary reasons for deploying these missiles in West Germany. First, when people asked why station missiles on German soil, aren't there enough nuclear bombs in the United States already to wipe out humanity many times over, the answer was: if the Soviets consider moving into Germany, they must know that they will eventually tread on missiles that will obviously not be trodden on, that will obviously not be removed, but that will be fired. That threat might not have been quite so clear if all missiles were stationed elsewhere, in the United States or on submarines. Second, those new Pershings and cruise missiles could reach the Soviet Union itself. Thus, the Soviets knew that they would definitely not be spared if ever they trod on West Germany—with the United States and the Chinese still out of it; aggression thus must seem too great a risk. Now those new missiles have been removed and only a few ancient short-range missiles are left. The signal to the Soviet Union now reads: if you attack West Germany only your satellites will suffer—unless the United States decides to use missiles that are not stationed in Germany and therefore must not "necessarily" be fired off in case of attack.

The question for us, then, is not: are the Americans to be trusted? It is, instead: do the Soviets expect the Americans to "mourir pour Bonn" if ever Bonn is threatened? If not, then World War III is a giant step closer de facto, unless we can satisfy ourselves that the climate in the Soviet Union has changed to a degree that makes practically any deterrence superfluous.

But there is now the clarion cry to "negotiate away all the missiles," raised by Foreign Minister Hans-Dietrich Genscher and other German strategists, meaning, of course, removing only the short-range missiles and thus "conventionalizing" defense. This would—

to a degree—remove the threat of atomic destruction from Germany and Western Europe. But would it also remove the threat of destruction per se? If the Soviet Union felt assured that in case of war there would be no atomic strike unless the United States were struck (or threatened) directly, Soviet leaders might very well feel that an attempt against West Germany carries no more risk than an attempt against Afghanistan—at worst, you get beaten back and lose many Soviet lives; this to be weighed by a political system that never was very conscious of Soviet or other lives. Again, you may consider whether this attitude has changed, unchangeably changed. The Soviet party program and the Soviet military doctrine have not yet changed.

There is always the question of whether you do the right thing at the right time. But aside from that, there are further complications. For one thing, Britain and France have made clear that they are not going to let their missiles be negotiated away so that their character as nuclear powers is lost while the Americans and the Soviets keep theirs. So, what would be the point of removing nuclear arms from the, well, glacis? For another thing, the Soviets are suddenly arguing that they cannot be made to keep only as many men, tanks, and planes as Western Europe has (plus a little something to threaten the Chinese). What about the U.S. ships, they ask. Can they not be used for attack? Explaining to them that a democracy under law never attacks offends their dignity as a superpower that wishes to be treated as an equal, not as an outlaw. And explaining to them that the United States has to protect its communications since, as mentioned earlier, Europe is not tucked in her continental underbelly, but very much exposed out front, and that the Soviets should be glad for having the advantage of the inner line, also leaves the Soviets unsatisfied because the world is today's battleground and he who holds the inner line can also complain that he is surrounded. The problem is not insoluble, but with the Soviet system being what it is, there are some lively rounds of negotiations to be expected.

CENTRAL EUROPE AND THE GERMAN QUESTION

Into all these complications the French have seen fit to introduce an explosive term: "Central Europe." At the Vienna talks they proposed out of a clear sky that Central Europe be considered an "object of special treatment" for the removal of armed forces. They probably did not mean any mischief. They probably felt that singling our Central Europe—West Germany, the Benelux states, East Germany, and some other Warsaw Pact regions—would leave their sovereignty and their missiles on the Plateau d'Albion unmolested by any superpower machinations. But it so happens that the term "Mitteleuropa," that is, Central Europe, is now being bandied about in West Germany, and the French, with the inconceivable lack of instinct that so often goes with their Cartesian clarte, have added a powerful and dangerous argument to it.

How dangerous it is becomes clear if a few explanatory words are added on the present German situation. When pundits hold forth on the German question it is often said that the West Germans feel a powerful reunification urge after more than 40 years of East–West partition and that they are therefore ready to make a deal with Gorbachev: trade in reunification for neutrality. You will also hear that the Germans are ready to forgo nuclear arms and possibly all arms because they see the vaterland as the battlefield of the future unless they disarm. Also, you hear that the Germans are tired of expiating Nazism and feel a nationalist urge coming on to assert themselves. So that, all in all, Germany is again becoming a point of nationalist unrest.

But all this is entirely wrong. There is no overwhelming urge in West Germany to give up the Western alliance. True, the majority of Germans want reunification. They want freedom for their East German fellow citizens. They feel that every country has the right to self-determination, so why shouldn't the Germans. If and when true self-determination strikes East Germany, everybody expects the East Germans to join the West Germans. But if for some reason the East Germans should decide to constitute their region as an independent state, nobody in West Germany would issue a call to arms. The ancient feeling that Germany must prove her greatness by owning more real estate is dead. Not even the Polish-occupied territories of Silesia, Pomerania, and East Prussia cause much comment these days; everybody expects an amicable solution once the Poles have their own freedom. The Germans do not like to be told that the Polish annexation of these territories and the partition of the rest of Germany must be accepted as penitence, as some people say, because that is absurdly outside of any precept of international law. But there are not territorial diehard crackpots in Germany anymore.

Yet the situation in Germany is volatile at the moment. If Germany now seems in jeopardy, the problem is not the people, it is the government, however well-meaning. To phrase it more charitably, there is a lack of intellectual leadership. The country was never wealthier, the people were never better off, the problems were never less pressing. We could have a red-green government in Bonn in the future, unless the Christian Democrats make a dramatic recovery in the polls or possibly in the elections for the European parliament.

It is a fact that the Germans who can vote red-green majorities into power and also support a rightist fringe party are the very same voters who gave Helmut Kohl a clear majority in 1983, after Kohl told them that he stood for deployment of medium-range missiles and for cutting budget expenditures. The voters have not changed, but the Christian Democrats have changed. The Social Democrats have already made one thing perfectly clear: if they come to power, there will be no modernization of short-range missiles. What will that mean for Germany's future in alliance, in the European Community (EC), in the West? Some Social Democrats think far beyond that. And that is where the scenarios praising the ancient concept of "Central Europe" (Mitteleuropa) come in.

The term Mitteleuropa was kicked about in the early days of World War I when there was a German empire and an Austro-Hungarian empire. Now the slogan forewarns of a far more sinister development. There are suggestions of close West German–East German "cooperation" or whatever, under some kind of "common roof," with thee Western powers as well as the Eastern powers withdrawing. If that comes about, then the epochal achievement of the first German chancellor, Konrad Adenauer—of leading the Germans out of their isolated central European position that twice led them into war— is likely to be reversed. This is because such a double Germany between the power blocs can hardly remain a member of NATO, any more than it can be a member of the European Community.

Germany as a "special" Central European entity—that is exactly what the new visionaries of Central Europe need. If it comes about, it is likely to bring a resurgence of nationalism, this time engineered by the same Social Democrats who have protested the nationalism of the "Republikaner" (the small Republican party of Germany). This may seem surprising because the Social Democrats have assailed alleged Christian Democrat nationalism over the asylum question because they hope to win voters, if ever foreigners are granted the franchise in West Germany. In the election campaign of 1983 they attacked Kohl for being "subservient to the Americans" and called for "defending the German interests."

So the Germans may very well undertake their third great Central European adventure within one century. If so, no one can foresee whither it will lead. One can only speculate how Kremlin hardliners might be encouraged to block reforms and bet on old recipes if Germany seems to be up for grabs after all.

How to avoid all this, how to stiffen the Christian Democrat's backbone and make them remember the virtues of an Adenauer or of the Kohl of 1983, I do not know. All I can offer Americans by way of advice is this: at least do not misjudge the Germans. Do not believe that just because certain politicians lose their nerve this means that "The Germans" are at it again. Do not believe the absurd speculation about a legitimate German "national interest" that would compel them to disarm unilaterally and give up NATO. The geostrategic situation has not changed, and what was right in the 1950s is right to this day. Besides, only recently a poll showed that the same Germans who rank Gorbachev far higher than any Western politician, including Reagan and Kohl, also feel—by about 76 percent—that military strength cannot yet be neglected. But the main point to be derived from all these differences and nervous reactions is this: that peace based merely on disarmament is an illusion and possibly leads into even greater risks. There is, in belief, no substitute for peace—for real security.

How to achieve it? Democracy, true democracy that reflects the will of the people, is the one simple and unfailing cure to all risks of war, terror, and destruction. Germans who used to condemn France as the archenemy and Britain as perfidious Albion do not even consider the possibility today that French or British missiles could be used to settle questions of trade restrictions or national greatness with them. And vice versa. But there are always those who ask, Can we foist our system, our western values on others?

This might be questionable if self-determination, the right of the people to handle their own business, were indeed a Caucasian specialty. But it is not. Dictators in Hanoi or Managua have tried to tell us that their people wish to go their own way. The people concerned never told us that. And I refuse to believe that there still are "lesser breeds without the law" who will tell you that it is their sovereign will not to have a sovereign will but to be led by some fuehrer. It is equally untenable to hold that certain nations are "not yet ripe for democracy," that, for instance, the Soviets must be subjected to what has been described as an "enlightened authoritarian regime" for yet a long time. The Russians are as civilized, as competent to handle their own affairs, as any Americans. Did not the American founding fathers, too, fear that the common people might prove too common, that an electoral college and God knows what other precautions were needed to make democracy a little less dependent on the demos? Well, it seems to work well in the United States, and apparently it works pretty well in two other countries where some people thought that it would take many years of teaching them how: West Germany and Japan. The Russians have had their veche, their ancient councils; the Ukranians have had their Rada in the republic "by the waterfalls" (za-porohy); Russians and Ukranians have voted in four elections to the Duma (the all-Russian parliament in St. Petersburg) since the reforms of 1906; both Russians and Ukranians established republics with free elections after the collapse of the czar's regime until the Bolsheviks smashed these. And now that they have been allowed at least some means of self-expression, the voting shows that the Russians, as well as the other nations in the Soviet Union, know very well how to use the suffrage.

REAGAN, *PERESTROIKA*, AND THE FUTURE

It is not an idle question whether President Reagan deserves any credit for *perestroika* or whether he was just lucky that it happened in his time. *Perestroika* is not the result of Communist shame over Communist oppression or crimes. *Perestroika* is not even the result of recognizing that Communism does not work, that the country is slowly falling apart unless free enterprise (which in effect means freedom) is introduced. The Soviets did fear that SDI (the Strategic

Defense Initiative) might work, that it might catapult the United States technically so far upward that the Soviet Union would be forced to acknowledge inferiority. But let me add that no less important was Reagan's insistence not only on numerical disarmament but on the human rights question. Even a regime like that in Moscow is sensitive to moral pressure. All this is not only important for Reagan's place in history; it is important to remember that Communism cannot and will not reform on its own; that it must be pressured from the outside if we want to avoid a relapse. There, then, lies peace—for no one fears that the Soviet people would form a lawless government if they can decide freely.

So the vista for democracy and the rule of law, of human rights, serves us as well as the Soviets, it provides a philosophy of peace on firmer ground than mere missile counting. And if we achieve the formation of a free Soviet Union with free enterprise; if the resources of this immeasurably rich country will be used as sensibly as are the resources of, say, North America; and if the other Eastern countries and China followed on the path to freedom and wealth—what would this mean for the hungry, miserable Third World if 1.5 billion people changed from poor to rich, from expansionist to helpful? All of this offers a hope to live for. Let us not only hope for it, let us press for it.

11

Gorbachev's Soviet Union

Martin Walker

One thing we tend to forget about the Soviet Union is just how enormously big it is and what the political implications of that can be. If you are Mikhail Gorbachev and you want to send orders to your man in Vladivostok, at any time when you are going to be in your Kremlin office you will be waking up the poor fellow in Vladivostok because he is 11 hours away in time. It used to be said of the British empire that it was an empire on which the sun never set. It can also be said that the sun doesn't really set on the Soviet Union. It is so big that there are 11 time zones from one end to the other, from the Baltic Sea to the Pacific Ocean.

There is a desert down on the Chinese frontier and on the Iranian frontier, and up in the north there is the Arctic. There is every conceivable kind of geology and of flora, apart from a tropical rain forest. The whole of the United States could pretty much get lost in the Soviet Union. And the size of it, I think as much as the climate, helps to shape the kind of difficulties that Gorbachev faces. For example, you cannot drive from one end of the Soviet Union to the other. There isn't actually a road that goes from Moscow across the Ural Mountains and through Siberia and across to the Pacific coast. There is one railroad line. This enormous size is one part of the problem that Gorbachev faces, but it is only the beginning.

The Soviet Union is a country where all of the factories are in the west, all of the raw materials are in the north and the east, and the only growing reservoir of people is down in the south, in Soviet Central Asia, where in fact, traditionally, they are Islamic peoples. Growth in the Soviet Union is going to involve either building the factories down where the people are, or taking the people to the factories, or taking the factories to the raw materials. Each one of those operations is going to be equivalent to reindustrializing the United States. It is a monstrous challenge, even where it is simply a challenge of economics and logistics. But it is also a challenge of cultures and nationalities, of tribal loyalties.

There are more than 120 official languages in the Soviet Union. As a Soviet citizen you would be within your rights to demand that your case be heard in court in one of those 120-odd languages. Newspapers and books are published in all of those languages, in spite of a constant campaign of Russification, which may look to us on the outside as a kind of cultural imperialism, but which from another point of view is a fairly inevitable way of trying to impose at least one single coherent structure upon such a diverse, multifarious, multiethnic state. In that sense, the Soviet Union remains an experiment just as much as it is a state.

OPTIMISM AND GLOOM

Like most of my Soviet friends, I wake up one morning feeling madly optimistic about Gorbachev's chances of democratizing, of humanizing that system. The next day, I wake up totally gloomy, convinced that he is going to be toppled in a Kremlin coup. And it seems to me that this state of manic depression about Gorbachev's chances is entirely typical of the way most Western observers, and most of the Soviet people, are feeling, because it is a time of unprecedented opportunity. It is a time of opposites, of great hopes mingled with great disappointments.

While I was working as a correspondent in the Soviet Union, *glasnost* began and the transformation was really quite astonishing. By the time I left the Soviet Union it was quite commonplace for Western journalists to be appearing on Soviet television as pundits or as debaters. I wrote a fairly regular column for one of the most *glasnost*–conscious newspapers, one called *Moskovy Novosti* or *Moscow News*.

I think that it was useful for them to be able to ask foreigners, Western correspondents, to do things that were just a little bit too dangerous for them at the time. For example, in 1986 I was able to run a column in *Moscow News* saying that it was time to build a memorial to the victims of Stalin's purges. About three months later, they actually founded a group, called Memorial, which was designed to do this. But in my discussions with the editor of *Moscow News* it was quite plain that he believed it was going to be easier for me to make the suggestion in his pages than for a Soviet journalist to do so. We were used, if you like, in the way that canaries are used by miners way down in pits. They'd say, "Well, if a foreigner can get away with this, maybe it's all right and we can try it next."

The nature of the story changed considerably while I was in the Soviet Union. When I first went to Moscow, basically there were two stories that we were expected to file. The first one was called "Power Struggle in the Kremlin," and the second one was called "Jewish Refuseniks Live in Hell." Basically, that was about 90 percent of the coverage coming out of Moscow for the Western press, and looking back, it wasn't necessarily a silly perspective.

As I have indicated, the story changed dramatically during the time I was there—there was *glasnost* in the newspapers, there was Moscow Spring, the astonishing surge of cultural revival and energy. However, I sometimes wonder whether we haven't given a bit of a wrong impression. There are only about 400 people who are foreign journalists accredited in Moscow, and about one-third of them are from mainstream Western news organizations like U.S. television and British newspapers. With a little bit of help from Mikhail Gorbachev, we managed to change the way in which the West perceived the Soviet Union. We began to report a very upbeat story: "*Glasnost* Success." Journalism is very susceptible to fashion, and I think this "gee whiz, isn't this wonderful" attitude has perhaps gone a little bit too far. My own gut feeling has varied between insane optimism and deep, despairing pessimism. This is what I mean about being manic depressive. You simply don't know which way things are going to turn out.

There are some things about the Soviet Union that make me very angry, and one of them is how it treats women. There are 280

million people in the Soviet Union. That means 140 million of them
are women. About half of them are of childbearing age, so that is
70 million women between the ages of 1 and 45. That means that
at any given moment in the Soviet Union, something like seven or
eight million women will be menstruating. The Soviet Union, a
superpower, a country that puts people into space and has deep
sea submarines that fire missiles that can obliterate the planet, cannot produce tampons or sanitary towels for its women. It regularly
goes through shortages of cotton wool. This, to me, is a symptom
of a fundamental lack of humanity, to fail to consider the needs of
half of the population.

There is also the fact that the standard form of birth control in
the Soviet Union is the abortion. The average Soviet woman, de-
pending on whose figures you take, has between four and seven
abortions in the course of her life. I mixed widely with Soviet
people, and I have yet to know one Soviet married woman who
has not had at least one abortion. Whatever stance you may take
on the issue of abortion, the point is that even if you believe in
abortion, one accepts that it creates an enormous psychological
trauma for the woman. And the Soviet Union simply refuses to spend
the money on producing birth-control pills, contraceptives, things
that we in the West take for granted. At the same time, although
the Soviet Union claims to have a decent public health-care system,
it is the women who bear the brunt of health care. You are a fool
if you go into a Soviet hospital and expect to eat the food that they
provide. You get your wife, your mother, your sister to bring your
food in. If you are going to the Soviet hospitals you had better take
in a bundle of one-ruble notes, otherwise you won't get any bed-
pans, you won't get any clean sheets, you won't get any towels, and
you will probably have to clean the area around your bed.

One of my best friends, a Soviet journalist, came to see me one
night in a considerable state of panic to say that his girlfriend was
bleeding badly. She had had an abortion in a state clinic, had left,
and had begun bleeding. she had gone back to the clinic, and she
had been given, in the usual Soviet way, a prescription for a drug.
Once the prescription is given with the drug mentioned on it, that
is the end of the Soviet medical services' responsibility. It is then
up to the individual to go and get that drug. You go to the chemist's
shop, and they will say, "No, we haven't got it." From that point

on, you turn to the black market. On that particular occasion, I spent four hours using my car to drive my friend around every aptyek (pharmacy) we could find in Moscow that was open, and then hanging around to wait for the black market to find us and see how desperate we were. Finally, we got the drug and it cost the usual sort of price in Moscow, a carton of Marlboros. The Soviet Union is the biggest black market state I have ever been in. Everything that is not nailed down is for sale, and then they will sell you the nails. To get an apartment, I, as a foreigner, found out who was the person to bribe, and I paid it. Most of us do. To get my Bolshoi tickets—no problem, a bottle of vodka or a bottle of whiskey to the manager would see to that. If I wanted a seat at a particularly good restaurant, again, whiskey, cigarettes. If you want to get into the Aragvi Restaurant off Gorky Street, and it is late at night and they claim to be closed, you hold up a packet of Marlboros against the door and you get straight in.

Something has to be done about this corruption and about the general level of despair that most Soviet people feel as they try to get by in a society that simply has almost none of the amenities that we all take for granted in the West. We are accustomed in the West to going into a supermarket any time of year and buying fresh fruit, fresh vegetables. In the Soviet Union throughout the winter months and the early spring months there simply are not any fruits in the state shops. There will be beetroot, there will be potatoes, there will be cabbages, some frost-blackened carrots, perhaps, but that is all unless you go to the free market. In the free market, tomatoes in January will cost 20 rubles a kilo, or $15 a pound. This, bear in mind, is in a city where the average monthly salary is 200 rubles. So, on 50 rubles a week, how many pounds of tomatoes are you going to buy? Now, sometimes you weaken. I can remember going into the Tsentralny Rinok, the central market in Moscow, in January and paying eight rubles, or $12, for a single cucumber because I wanted to have that crunch, that taste of green.

The Soviet Union simply has not yet found a way to feed itself. In 1988 it imported 36 million tons of U.S. grain. This was in a country that before the revolution was a major and regular exporter of wheat. At the free markets, the peasants sell the crops that come from their private plots, which are really just very large black gardens. These plots take up 3 percent of the arable land in the Soviet

Union and produce about 30 percent of the food because people have the incentive to grow things.

NEEDED REFORMS

There are three main reforms, I think, that have to take place in the Soviet economy if Gorbachev is to have a chance. And most Western observers—and, indeed, most Soviet economists—will agree on what they are. One of the reasons why they are often so pessimistic about Gorabachev's chances is that for all of the marvelous things he has done in foreign policy and in cultural liberation, he has consistently ducked and avoided the main reforms on the economic front. The three reforms that I believe are absolutely necessary are based on the problem of dismantling state control of the economy.

The first of these reforms would be to abolish the food subsidies that keep Soviet bread, for example, so cheap. It is cheaper for the peasants to feed their livestock, their private pigs or cattle, on bread, than to buy fodder—that is how cheap bread is. Gorbachev once complained in a speech that he saw boys playing football with loaves of bread.

Bread is not the only problem. It costs the Soviet state about five-and-a-half rubles a kilo to produce meat, and it is sold in the state stores for two rubles a kilo. Wonderful, you might say. Except what this means is that you can hardly ever find meat in the state stores. It is sold out of the back door, on the black market. The current cost to the state budget of food subsidies on meat and milk and bread alone is about 70,000 billion rubles a year, which is more than three times what the Soviets admit to spending on defense. Somehow, that has got to be ended because it is distorting the entire production and investment structure of the economy. It is also encouraging further distortions in the national wage structure. It encourages the Soviet Union to continue as a low-wage economy, and that is quite a bad thing.

The second reform that the Soviets have to bring about, I think, is to bring the country into the world economy by making the ruble into a convertible currency; in other words, floating the ruble against the dollar and other hard currencies. Officially, in a bank, you pay about $1.50 for each ruble that you buy. On the black market, you will get three or four and more rubles for every dollar. In other words, there is about a 600 or 700 percent difference in real value. This explains why Soviet cars, the Soviet-made Ladas, are so enormously cheap in the West. In Britain, Soviet-made Ladas sell for around about $4,000, as cheap as you can get. It is probably worth about that much, but it costs them a great deal more to produce it. I think that the Soviet fear that their ruble will collapse if they do float it on the Western market is perhaps a bit overstated. After all, the Soviet Union is the world's biggest producer of energy, of oil, and it is the world's second biggest producer of gold. Any economy backed by those two commodities should not be in too much bad shape.

The third needed reform is ending price controls, which I think are probably the most damaging single feature of the entire command economy. Soviet factories do not add up their costs of raw materials and production and then add in their profit and fix their prices accordingly, because every single input price in the Soviet economy is entirely fiction. They do not pay for the cost of the land or for the cost of the investment in new plant or new machinery, and they do not pay any kind of realistic cost for the energy, the electricity, and the gas that they consume. All of this means that Soviet managers are living in a kind of Alice-in-Wonderland state. An example of what this means in reality is that every year the Soviet Union is losing its best agricultural land because it is cheap to build a dam in a river valley. River valleys tend to be good and fertile land. But because the land does not cost anything in the Soviet Union, nobody has to work out what it costs to buy the land or to forgo the crops if a dam is going to be built across a river. There is no economic logic. There is no market to indicate what the trade-off is in value between the electricity produced by the dam and the amount of land and crops that are given up in order to put that dam there. Until the concept of rent, of what is actually being paid for the use of land, comes into the Soviet economy, Gorbachev does not have a chance.

The Soviets have a saying, "They pretend to pay us and we pretend to work." Soviet productivity is desperately low, because what are the workers working for? The average income in Moscow is 200 rubles a month. A Lada car will cost 11,500 rubles, about four years' earnings. Even then, there is a wait of two-and-a-half to three years.

There is not any real prospect of an ordinary Soviet worker saving up to buy a car. There is not much point in saving up to buy a television set because the biggest single cause of fires in Soviet homes is the tendency of Soviet television sets to explode regularly.

It is true that Soviet citizens pay very little for an apartment, 10 or 15 rubles a month, and that food is subsidized. But there is nothing in the shops to really spend money on, and the result is that Soviet savings banks have something like 300 billion rubles stored up in them. It makes them by far the thriftiest people in the world after the Japanese. It makes Americans with their credit cards look like spendthrifts, but Americans have things in their shops that they want to buy, and the Soviets do not. And because there is nothing they want to buy, there are no incentives. What is the point of working harder in the Soviet Union?

These economic reforms, which I think will come, are going to come amid a great deal of political upheaval and unrest and diffi- culty. We are already seeing a kind of class distinction emerging in the Soviet Union between people on less-than-average wages, who desperately need those food subsidies, and the people who earn a great deal more. When Leonid Brezhnev talked about the Soviet Union as a workers' state, he wasn't talking through his hat. They have had a curious reversal of the ordinary white collar—blue collar relationship that we have in the West. The Soviets will often tell you that they do not have discrimination against women because 70 percent of their doctors are women and 70 percent of their teachers are women. What they do not tell you is that they have deskilled, devalued, those jobs. The average Soviet doctor's pay is about 140 rubles a month, less than the average income. The av- erage teacher's pay is about the same because these are jobs held by women; therefore, the salaries can be held down.

The average blue-collar worker, on the other hand, tends to be rather better off. The average take-home pay of a coal miner in the Donetsk Basin in the Ukraine is about 320 to 340 rubles a month. Which would you rather be, a Soviet doctor after five or six years of training, or a Donetsk coal miner? Certainly, in terms of the income result, a coal miner. However, this disparity between the blue collar and the white collar is being distorted by a new kind of NEP (New Economic Program).

In the 1920s, when Lenin tried to make the Soviet economy

recover from the civil war by introducing a touch of capitalism, it was called the New Economic Policy, or NEP. And the new private traders, who rented licenses and began to get commerce going again, were called the "Nepmen." They were widely hated because they were rich and they were able to throw expensive and lavish parties in restaurants and drive around in cars. The Nepmen have cast a painful shadow upon the very image of commercial enterprise in the Soviet Union ever since. Many of the new people who are making money out of the fledgling co-operatives that Gorbachev has allowed to open up are deeply worried that what happened to the Nepmen could happen to them, too. In fact, a friend of mine who runs one of the new co-op restaurants in Moscow said that the reason why his prices were so high was that he reckoned he only had three or four years to make his pile before it would all go back to normal again.

There is, however, another factor in this class mix between the very rich and the poor doctors and the poor teachers, and it is a much more hopeful sign. It is a sign that makes me think that perhaps Gorbachev is going to make it after all.

BUILDING EDUCATION AND THE MIDDLE CLASS

It is important to remember that the Soviet Union is a country that has regularly beheaded itself. Look back in this century: in 1914 World War I began and in 1917 the revolution took place. Those two events, between them, managed to wipe out the old czarist governing class—the officer corps, the civil servants, the landowners. They were all killed in the war or in the revolution or were expelled afterward.

Then, in the 1920s, the old Bolsheviks somehow had to knock together a new official class, a new governing class. And they did so. They put together an administrative structure, but in the 1930s Stalin came along and beheaded it yet again. We should not forget that the first victims of Stalin's purges were the party officials. At the same time that Stalin beheaded this Soviet official class in the 1930s, he also wiped out the dreaming class—the poets, the writers, the artists. Having cut the head off the Soviet Union, he also ripped its soul out as well. And then came World War II, when 20 million

Soviets died. I think that it is a toss-up whether Hitler or Stalin killed more Russians, but certainly it is true that World War II was a devastating loss to the Soviet Union. In the Republic of Georgia, for example, of men born between the years of 1921 and 1924, the ones in the peak fighting age for World War II, only three percent survived. In the city of Leningrad there is a cemetery, a huge field with half a dozen big mounds in it, and each of those mounds represents a year. In that one cemetery 650,000 people are buried. That is more than the United States and Britain together lost in World War II, and that was in one city.

Since 1945, however, the Soviet Union has had more than 40 years of peace. There has been a huge investment in education. Mikhail Gorbachev, born on a farm in the Northern Caucuses, was given the chance by the Soviet Union, by the Soviet education system, to go to Moscow University, to go to law school. Gorbachev is one of the 1.4 million lawyers turned out by Soviet law schools in the years since 1955. They have rebuilt their official class. They have rebuilt an intellectual class, an intelligentsia. The Soviet Union has a fine educational system. It is the politics that have been wrong and the economics that have been wrong.

If you go to a meeting in a Soviet university you will find people who are well read. I was constantly humbled by how much better Soviets knew Shakespeare than I did. There is nothing wrong with the brains at all, and there is nothing wrong with the educational system. What is wrong is the political system that has held them down for so long. And I think that the 40 years without war that they have had since the end of World War II has helped to produce not just Gorbachev, but an entire generation like him.

What we are seeing with Gorbachev is the emergence of a new middle class that has decided that the time has come for dramatic, fundamental, generational change. When we listen to Mikhail Gorbachev's speeches, what I am referring to is evident. These people are not from another planet. They don't have horns. Seventy years of the Soviet system have not created the anti-Christ. They are people who are laboring under an appallingly inefficient structure.

GORBACHEV AND THE SOVIET PARADOX

The cause of my manic depression about the future in the Soviet Union, the optimism and the despair, came together for me when

Gorbachev made his quite dramatic speech at the United Nations in December 1988. Journalists are taught that we have got to get the main story into the first paragraph. In covering that speech, we focused upon the fact that he announced troop cuts of 500,000 men from the Soviet army and the withdrawal of six tank divisions from Eastern Europe. However, looking more deeply into that speech, what Gorbachev was really trying to talk about was a new world order, of which these troop cuts were just symptoms. He was talking about the old logic of international relations as a zero-sum game in which when I lose, you win or when I win, you lose. Gorbachev was saying that time has to come to an end:

The formula of our development at the expense of others must be on the way out. In the light of existing realities, no genuine progress is possible at the expense of the rights and freedoms of individuals and of nations, nor at the expense of nature. The world of the arms race had involved our living through a paradox where an increase in the numbers of weapons didn't make nations safer, but it made the world a more dangerous place for everybody.[1]

Gorbachev cut the umbilical cord to seven decades of Communist orthodoxy and he consigned the 1917 revolution to history, an event to be compared with the French Revolution of 1789—two revolutions that shaped the way of thinking that is still prevalent in social consciousness, but are now historical events. Gorbachev abandoned the concept of the international power struggle:

Today, we have entered an era when progress will be shaped by universal human interests. Further world progress is only possible through a search for universal human consensus as we move forward to a new world order. We have concluded that we should jointly seek the way leading to the supremacy of the universal human idea over the endless multitude of centrifugal forces. This is the only way to preserve the vitality of this human civilization, possibly the only one in the entire universe.[2]

This was statesmanship of an astonishing boldness and vision and ambition, an attempt to speak for the entire planet, to make the case on behalf of human civilization rather than for the economically wretched but military superpower that he actually led. And yet, as this brave new world he spoke of dawned the next day, what did we see but Gorbachev's features sagging with grief as he spoke at the airport in New York before flying home to the Armenian earthquake. Now, that was an event on the same massive scale as so many things Soviet or Russian. The sufferings of that country always seem greater, just as its novels are always longer, as though the tragedies and also the achievements are inevitably condemned to take place on a grand superhuman scale that baffles the imagination of the rest of us.

The Armenian earthquake was a monstrous disaster that wrung the hearts of humanity. Yet, as *Isvestia* asked a week after the earthquake happened, "Can anyone doubt that if this same earthquake had happened in California and not in our country, the death toll would have been 1,000 or even less and the homeless would have been sheltered within the first day?" There were apartment houses built of shoddy concrete, reinforcement rods that workers had never bothered to weld together, and the famous civil defense machine that we were warned about proved never to exist when tested by natural disaster.

The Soviet Union is a superpower, yet rescuers were still digging with their bare hands ten days after the shock. Such incompetence is a savage indictment of the Soviet system. However, I am afraid that it is all too typical. The sheer incompetence of the Soviet system in responding to the emergency in Armenia was just as revealing of Soviet reality as any Gorbachev speech.

NOTES

1. Excerpts from Mikhail S. Gorbachev's speech to the United Nations General Assembly, *New York Times*, December 8, 1988.
2. Ibid.

12

Dr. Zhivago and Mr. Gorbachev

Harold D. Piper

Po Rossii mchitsa troika:
Raika, Mishka, perestroika

A Soviet friend of mine gave me some examples of the doggerel Muscovites are exchanging. First of all, of course, it was amazing that I was talking to this woman at all. We were in a comfortable, rambling white house in bucolic horse country north of Baltimore. She was visiting her cousin; a few days later she went back to Moscow. Such a thing was unthinkable only two or three years ago—that Soviet citizens could travel abroad like any other people, and go home again, and maybe visit again next year, or whenever time and money allow. "I'll bet you're a fan of *perestroika*," I said to her,

"I am, yes," she replied, "but not many of my friends are." And she recited, in the sing-song that makes Russian children's poems so charming:

Po Rossii mchitsa troika:
Raika, Mishka, perestroika:

"Russia's driven by a troika:
Raika, Raisa, Mishka, Mikey Gorbachev, perestroika."
Po Rossii mchitsa troika:
Raika, Mishka, perestroika.

And here's another one: Lyonichka, druzhochek—That's Lenny, Lenny Brezhnev, and this must surely be the unique example in contemporary Soviet culture of nostalgia for Leonid Brezhnev:

Lyonichka, druzhochek, otkroi glazkil
Nyet in vodki, ni kolbaski
Etot lysyu demagog
Sperestroikoi bcex zayob

Let's clean it up in translation:

Lenny, pal, you've heard the News?
There's no more sausage, no more booze
It's that chromedome Gorbo's doing
Perestroika—royal screwing.

And one more:

Perestroika—mat' rodnaya,
Khozraschot—otets rodnoi
Na khui mne sem'ya takaya
Luche budu sirotoi.

Perestroika's my mother, *khozraschot* is my father. *Khozraschot* is a basic economic reform, literally "self-financing mechanism," and I don't mind telling you, "self-financing mechanism" is a bear to translate into a line of doggerel.

Perestroika whelped me,
Sired by bottom line.
These my folks?—God help me!
Would an orphan's life were mine.

We speak of Gorbachev as a man on a tightrope. Will he go too far? Will Ligachev trip him up? Where do the army and the KGB stand on *perestroika*? I'm sure these are important questions, but if you want to assess the prospects for *perestroika*, perhaps instead of looking at the top of Soviet society, we should look at the bottom. If *perestroika* dies, the assassin may not be the deadwood bureaucracy or an ambitious rival, but the priterpelost of the ordinary Soviet citizen.

ENDURANCE AND HUMILIATION

"Priterpelost" is not in the dictionary. Yevgeny Yevtushenko came up with the word. A relative had brought him a May Day gift of a small packet of sugar. Sugar, of course, had disappeared from Soviet shelves during Gorbachev's campaign against alcohol: the sugar got commandeered by moonshiners. But Yevtushenko's relative wasn't thinking about any particular Gorbachev policy when she sighed about the persistent shortages of what should be everyday items: "This is what we have come to; it's all because of our having become inured to these things—damn "priterpelost."

Endurance, Yevtushenko remarks, is a heroic quality that the Soviet people rightly pride themselves on. Priterpelost is something else—a passive acceptance, or surrender to the force of habit. The word is a back-formation from "priterpetsya," to become inured to something, as a blacksmith's hands can tolerate heat. And the Soviet people, Yevtushenko says, have become inured to so much that they have lost the habit of fighting back, of asserting themselves, of refusing to tolerate what ought to be intolerable. Whose fault is it that there is no sugar? Why, the Central Committee's, of course, and the Council of Ministers. But also, he said, our own: "We have become inured to the disappearance of first one item and then another. Should one be surprised at this, when we once tolerated the disappearance of people?"

In one of his own poems, "Bratsk Hydroelectric Power Station," Yevtushenko asks of the Soviet Union and all that it has endured: "How did she endure her own endurance?" These words, he said, were written in a sort of "breathless, emotional delight" at his people's endless capacity for long and patient suffering. But one night Yevtushenko heard an actress recite them in angry outrage at the slavish passivity of an endurance that is the cause of so many of the Soviet Union's misfortunes—and Yevtushenko acknowledged that his verse contained a truth that he himself had never recognized.

That was Yevtushenko in 1988. In 1989 Soviet citizens went to the polls. What do the astonishing results tell us about priterpelost? Eighty-nine percent for Yeltsin: Is this a passive people whose timidity keeps them enslaved? Party bosses running unopposed, defeated anyway because more than half the voters crossed their names off the ballot. Is this a hopeless, conformist society of untermenschen incapable of self-government?

I'm afraid I am not yet ready to abandon Yevtushenko's concept of priterpelost; but perhaps it is time to add a second idea from another poet, Boris Pasternak, who wrote of "the abyss of humiliation."

If the Soviet people create many of their own problems by permitting themselves to "endure their own endurance," one reason, surely, is that priterpelost is the appropriate response to the "abyss of humiliation" that has characterized daily life in Russia throughout the Soviet period.

It is humiliating for a married couple to have to live with their in-laws for perhaps ten years because there are too few apartments. It is humiliating to have to queue up for shoddy goods. It is humiliating that the Soviet Union cannot feed itself and depends on the capitalist world for its calories. It is humiliating that rationing should be in effect in many areas of the country 44 years after the war ended and in the seventy-second year of Soviet power. Humiliating that in the midst of the several billion trees of Siberia there should be a paper shortage. Humiliating that Soviets should be denied foreign travel—and should be denied even in their own country the right to reside wherever they wish. Humiliating that plain sugar should be a treasured May Day gift. When I lived in Moscow, one winter it was onions. An onion for New Year's would really impress your sweetie, people joked, but if you should present it wrapped in toilet paper... ooh-la-la, there would be no limit to her gratitude. Candy is dandy, but liquor is quicker; whereas an onion wrapped in toilet paper... Wow! Humiliating! A recent front-page headline in *Izvestia* read, "Will there be enough potatoes?" Potatoes? Humiliating.

And what is most humiliating, of course, is the incessant Panglossian incantation that the Soviet Union is somehow in the vanguard of peoples, that one bright day everybody will get to live like the Soviets. No, maybe even more humiliating than that is the insulting paternalism that insists that the Soviet people must be looked after because they are incapable of thinking for themselves. What makes this so humiliating is that this perception so often seems to be shared by the people themselves. I will cite a couple of examples.

Valentin Zorin is a prominent Soviet television commentator. Once, just for devilment, I made him a proposition. At the time—10 or 12 years ago—there was a brand new news-interview show on Hungarian television that actually allowed mainstream Western journalists to comment in an uncontrolled setting on current events. Tony Collings of *Newsweek* was the first American to appear. He said they played it pretty straight. There was a Soviet journalist to contradict everything Tony said, and the Soviet journalist got to speak last. But the important thing was that for the first time, uncensored Western viewpoints were being heard on Hungarian television. I said to Zorin, "Why not do a program like that here in Moscow? Why not have me on your show? We could talk about world peace, or the obligation of Soviet and U.S. citizens to jointly work for the mutual drawing together of peoples—anything you like."

Well, I knew Zorin wasn't about to fall into this trap, but his answer did surprise me.

"You know," he said, "I really wish I could do that. I was the one who encouraged this Hungarian to open up his show, and I'd love to do the same here. But let me tell you why it would never work in the Soviet Union." I smiled knowingly, and he shook his head. "No, I have the freedom to do it, they wouldn't stop me. But the Soviet people are simply not ready for such a show." As my grin broadened to a smirk, he told me a little story.

Not too long ago, he said, he had done a show on something not very controversial, and certainly not ideologically sensitive. It was about farming, about when is the best time to plant, and which varieties of wheat do best in various climates. He had two agricultural experts on the program—and they disagreed. One said that the lower yield of one variety of wheat was offset by its greater hardiness, making it more suitable for cultivation in Central Russia, and the other said, no, if you plant it two weeks later, the higher-yielding will survive... and so on.

Anyway, he said that show got more mail than anything else he had ever done. And all of it was negative! "You didn't tell us which so-called expert was right." They were not just confused, they were angry. "How are we supposed to know whom to believe? Why do you do a show that has no point? What is the use of raising a question if you don't tell us the answer?"

He said, "I could put you on my show … today. We don't have to talk about the responsibilities of journalists for drawing together the peoples—we could talk about arms control, or so-called human rights. But the thing is, you know we wouldn't agree, and then the people would be frustrated. From my show they expect to know the truth. They don't understand your American idea that everything's relative, that what may be true for you is not necessarily true for me. It is my responsibility to explain to them what they are to believe about arms and human rights, and the responsibilities of journalists—and even about which crops to plant in cold weather. I tell you, the Soviet people are not ready for a debate such as you propose."

Well, of course Comrade Zorin was quite serious. I am quite sure he really did get a lot of angry mail after his program on agriculture. And more to the point, he sees himself not as a medium of information that the people will evaluate and use, guided by their common senses, but as a steward of the truth, which he husbands as a trustee of the people, and which he disburses to the people according to their needs … as the vanguard determines what those needs may be.

Another example. I was interviewing an official of the Soviet writers' union, for a story about Soviet literature. He named this one and that one as giants of the contemporary literary scene. And pretty soon I felt the need to needle him as I had needled Zorin. "These are all excellent writers," I said, "and yet, it is said that the Soviet Union's greatest writer is none of these, but Alexander Solzhenitsyn, whose voice is silenced in his homeland."

The official started to squirm and explain to me that Solzhenitsyn is not only scum but also dregs. And I interrupted him and said, "None of this do I dispute. Scum—perhaps. Dregs—entirely possible. And yet why should not even Solzhenitsyn have the right to speak? If, as you say and I believe, the average Soviet citizen is too patriotic and too sensible to believe what this scum-and-dregs

Solzhenitsyn writes, then what harm is done? We suffer a child to babble nonsense; why not also suffer a fool, even a friend? Will not the truth protect us even from such as Solzhenitsyn?" And he told me a little story.

This literary official was an older man, and he had served in World War II as an officer. One bitter day in the winter of 1943 he was somewhere in the Baltics. The war was not going well. The Germans occupied vast areas of the Soviet Union. Far to the southeast a life-and-death battle rated at the Volga River city named Stalingrad. He and his company were advancing through a town where there had been hard fighting. They had the Germans on the run, but they had to be wary of pro-Nazi partisan collaborators.

Suddenly a man in an officer's uniform—a Soviet officer's uniform—appeared on a second-story balcony directly in front of the captain and his weary men. "Stalingrad has fallen," the officer shouted. "We are lost, all is lost!"

The literary official, telling me the story 35 years later said, "I immediately drew my pistol and shot the man dead. Did I know who the man was? No! He could have been a Nazi collaborator spreading lies, or maybe he really was a Soviet officer genuinely mistaken.... Or perhaps Stalingrad really had fallen. I had no way of knowing. But I knew this—I knew that my men, exhausted after days of heavy fighting, did not need to hear this news. It would have demoralized them utterly. So I shot the man on the balcony." Time enough later to inquire whether Stalingrad had or had not fallen.

That struck me as rather a remarkable explanation. Solzhenitsyn, then, is the man on the balcony. This is no time for caviling like Pilate about what is truth. The people were so exhausted by war, so vulnerable to confusion and sabotage, that to protect them we had to shoot first—shoot the man on the balcony. Later on we'll find out whether he's telling the truth, and if so, we'll integrate it gently into our message to the Soviet people—so that they'll never be left not knowing what to think.

Yes, everybody knows that this is what the Soviet Union has been—priterpelost or slavish endurance, humiliation, paternalism, manipulation. The question is, Is the Soviet Union now becoming something different? Does the 1989 election mark a new assertiveness on the part of the narod, is it beginning to feel its power?

Certainly, the vote was a stunning message of alienation and polarization, a challenge across the "abyss of humiliation." Whether that is the first step toward civic virtue and political maturity is what I question. When 89 percent of the voters back a candidate, it sounds to me suspiciously like an election run by Communists, even though in this case it was a mirror-image vote, 89 percent rejecting the progressive revolutionary vanguard.

OLD MYTHS AND THE ERA OF STAGNATION

Back in what we now call the Era of Stagnation, I wrote the obituary of Leonid Brezhnev that my paper, the *Baltimore Sun*, kept in type, to be rushed into print upon his death. By the time he finally died, I was in Germany, and the obit had been rather extensively rewritten and updated by my successor. But it contained roughly the same judgments of the Brezhnev era, and since I do not claim brilliance or originality, I can say with some assurance that my judgments represented the distillation of enlightened academic and journalistic opinion at the time—the opinion of the reasonable Kremlinologists. And what we reasonable Kremlinologists said was the Brezhnev represented a pause for consolidation after the turmoil of Stalin and the impetuosity of Khrushchev. Not just a pause for consolidation—that is another name for the Era of Stagnation—but a needed pause for consolidation. It is a relief to note that I did say that problems were piling up that Brezhnev's successors were going to have to deal with, some of them quite knotty problems indeed.

But on the whole, the judgment of us reasonable Kremlinologists was that the Brezhnev era had been, in Soviet terms, a success. The country had achieved full military parity with the United States. Although it had grave economic problems, living standards were advancing nevertheless, as betokened by the first rudimentary traffic jams and parking problems of a Soviet "Automobile Age," slightly more stylish couture on promenade between acts at the Bolshoi Ballet, and a gradual substitution of gristly meat and wormy vegetables for bread and potatoes in the Soviet diet. And most important, under Brezhnev there was the beginning of something resembling the concept of process.

Today we call it the dead hand of reactionary bureaucracy, but only ten years ago we reasonable Kremlinologists viewed it as a positive development that the apparat had some security of tenure. Not having to worry about being abducted in the night and shot, officials were free to do their jobs, to use their competence—even, perhaps, to show some initiative. Brezhnev may have stopped the cultural thaw and imprisoned many dissidents, but still, it had to be said that people were no longer afraid to get indignant about things. This was progress. There was debate in *Problems of Communism* and other publications about whether this collective indignation might amount, in time, to the beginnings of a public opinion that the leadership would have to regard. Some said there already was a de facto public opinion.

At any rate, we all believed that even if the Soviet Union did have a free election, things might not change all that much. Kosygin might beat Brezhnev, but so what? In a free election matching Brezhnev with, say, Andrei Sakharov, we all thought Brezhnev probably would win—first of all because he could control ward-level patronage, but second—and more important—because the Soviet people, like most people, having learned to make do with what they've got, are too conservative to vote for really radical change. And maybe we were right, maybe it would have been that way in free elections held at that time, because there was no *glasnost* then to give voice to discontent and help protesters to link up.

What was wrong with our reasoned and reasonable analysis of the Soviet Union under Brezhnev and of the virtues of stability? Why did we not recognize the depth of Soviet alienation? For one thing, we wanted to be levelheaded, we didn't want to go off half-cocked. Many of us didn't want to engage in polemics about whether this really was an evil empire, the "focus of evil in the modern world."

Then too, take those doggerel verses I cited—*Po Rossii mchitsa troika*. I took them as good-natured expressions of a real frustration, but an inchoate frustration—one that wasn't going anywhere and wasn't intended to go anywhere. I was convinced that, although demoralized and sullen, the Soviets were not about to revolt. Yet, what happened in the March 1989 elections? Out of the "abyss of humiliation," they hit back. They hit back as we never could have imagined in the Era of Stagnation. But does it really mean that they've thrown off their priterpelost, the all-enduring passivity that

Yevtushenko complains of? And even if they have, the more important question is whether the Soviet people have suddenly developed the civic virtues Gorbachev is counting on to bring off *perestroika*. I think we need one more visit to Pasternak, to Dr. Zhivago, and his distinction between the mentalities of the Old Testament and New Testament.

THE INDIVIDUAL AND SOCIETY

Dr. Zhivago believed that the tragedy of the Russian revolution was that it had repealed 1,900 years of human spiritual progress and flung a New Testament nation back into an Old Testament mentality. Now, this is a religious metaphor, but as it struck Dr. Zhivago, it is not really about religion; rather, it is a political, or psychological, or psycho-spiritual observation. Certainly it is not about the alleged superiority of Christianity to Judaism, because for one thing, Judaism itself is no longer a set of taboos.

Dr. Zhivago was particularly taken with the discourse of Sima Tuntseva and returned to her ideas, elaborating on them. Tribal religion, Tuntseva said, was collective. God's covenant was made with Israel as a people, and as a people Israel flourished or failed. There were, of course, good and bad people in those times, but their individual virtues and sins went into the scorebook on behalf of the whole people. Over and over, we are told of the nation losing a battle or suffering a famine because of corporate sins. The nation was guided by magicians who could part the seas, turn a stick into a serpent, and divine God in a burning bush. Most important, the magician had exclusive access to the sacred laws that rule human conduct; God spoke directly only to the prophet elite, which then passed the message on to the people—who were expected, at their corporate peril, to obey.

The new covenant, however, is between God and the individual. Each man and woman has God's commandments written on his heart, each is personally responsible to exercise his or her personal spiritual sense. Each sin stains the sinner alone; each man or woman may accept God's grace—through his own faith, not through righteousness imputed to members of a group, or through the exertions of a priestly caste.

Now, it is vital to repeat that I am not, and Zhivago was not, explaining why Christianity is a better religion than Judaism. You could just as well compare twentieth-century Judaism with first-century Christianity and point out, quite validly, that Judaism is more rational, less credulous, less supernatural than Christianity. I say again, this comparison is not about religion, but about the relation between the individual and society. Does the individual find meaning as a member of a corporate or collective body; or is he a free moral agent, personally and individually responsible to God or to history?

In our century we incline to the latter view, to what Zhivago called the New Testament view, that God covenants with us as individuals, not as peoples. And that is why Zhivago believed that the Communists were a spiritual anachronism, that they had rolled Russia back to the Old Testament, to the time when individual men and women were subsumed into collectives that were corporately damned (e.g., the bourgeoisie, the independent kulak farmers) or corporately redeemed (e.g., the proletariat). Suddenly in 1917, for the first time since the Romans, Zhivago said, a magical priesthood had sprung up, the Communists, the people's vanguard, who long knew the "Iron Laws of History" and exacted the people's obedience to them.

The Communist Revolution marked the return of "the reign of numbers . . . the duty, imposed by armed force, to live unanimously as a people." People have lost confidence, Dr. Zhivago said, in the value of their own opinions. "People imagined that it was out of date to follow their own moral sense, that they must all sing in chorus, and live by other people's notions, notions that were being crammed down everybody's throat." Civilization had seen nothing like it, Dr. Zhivago suggested, since the fall of the Roman Empire. But now the Old Testament had returned—in the name of progress.

I am less certain than Dr. Zhivago that Russia ever had left the Old Testament. Eighty-nine percent for Yeltsin sounds suspiciously like a people still "living unanimously as a people," still "all singing in chorus" and living by somebody's notions that have suddenly gotten into everybody's throats at the same time. Zhivago and his Westernized, intellectual friends were New Testament people, of course, but they were only a fraction of the narod. The 1917 revolution came scarcely 50 years after the freeing of the serfs. Many historians have suggested that authoritarian socialism, so-called, succeeded in Russia to the extent it did because it did not require much uprooting of the old feudal structure, but only of the tender "bourgeois" plants that hardly had time to get established. Yevtushenko himself has suggested that Soviet history has been a process of negative selection, in that by eliminating all creativity, all independent thinking, the Communist leadership has been breeding selectively for docility, for priterpelost!

But Gorbachev seems to be betting the other way, betting that there are enough New Testament souls in the Soviet Union—men and women who can be appealed to as individuals, who can be reasoned with, who will accept responsibility—to bring off *perestroika*. We speak of him as a man on a tightrope, but I suggest he is really the Man on the Balcony, the man in my story about the literary bureaucrat. "Stalingrad has fallen," shouts the Man on the Balcony. A metaphorical Stalingrad: "The economy is in ruins, our society has stagnated, our political life is built on lies. All is lost, unless. . . ."

We know what happened to the original Man on the Balcony. Our brave lieutenant litterateur shot him for the good of the demoralized troops. Gorbachev may escape that fate. But it might happen that in this replay of the story, he will end up being stricken from the balcony by the troops themselves—having thrown off their priterpelost without, as yet, having developed the self-restraint and individual discipline, the civic virtues, required for what Zhivago saw as New Testament citizenship. I am sure Gorbachev is aware of this danger, the danger not from ambitious rivals, but from the people below. *Perestroika* is going to take—ironically enough—the creation of something we haven't heard much about in recent years: The New Soviet Man.

Bibliography

Adelman, Jonathan R., and Debora A. Palmieri. *Dynamics of Soviet Foreign Policy*. New York: Harper and Row, 1988.

Allison, Graham T., and William L. Ury, eds. *Windows of Opportunity: From the Cold War to Peaceful Competition in the U.S.–Soviet Relations*. New York: Ballinger, 1989.

Arbatov, Georgi, and Willem Oltmans. *The Soviet Viewpoint*. New York: Dodd, Mead and Company, 1983.

Aslund, Anders. *Gorbachev's Struggle for Reform*. Ithaca, N.Y.: Cornell University Press, 1989.

Babbage, Ross. *The Soviets in the Pacific in the 1990s*. Elmsford, N.Y.: Pergamon, 1989.

Bahry, Donna. *Outside Moscow: Power, Politics, and Budgetary Policy in the Soviet Republics*. New York: Columbia University Press, 1987.

Baradat, Leon. *Soviet Political Society*. 2d ed. Englewood Cliffs, N.J.: Prentice-Hall, 1988.

Bernstein, Jerome S. *Power and Politics: The Psychology of Soviet–American Partnership*. Boston, Ma.: Shambhala, 1989.

Bialer, Seweryn. *The Soviet Paradox: External Expansion, Internal Decline*. New York: Random House, 1987.

Bialer, Seweryn, ed. *Politics, Society and Nationality inside Gorbachev's Russia*. Boulder, Co.: Westview, 1989.

Bialer, Seweryn, and Michael Mandelbaum, eds. *Gorbachev's Russia and American Foreign Policy*. Boulder, Co.: Westview, 1988.

Bittman, Ladisla, ed. *The New Image-Makers: Soviet Propaganda and Disinformation Today*. Elmsford, N.Y.: Pergamon, 1988.

Black, Cyril E. *Understanding Soviet Politics: The Perspective of Russian History*. Boulder, Co.: Westview, 1986.

Blacker, Coit D. *Reluctant Warriors: The United States, the Soviet Union, and Arms Control*. New York: W. H. Freeman, 1987.

Bradley, Bill, et al. *Implications of Soviet New Thinking*. Boulder, Co.: Westview, 1988.

Brown, Archie, and Michael Kaser, eds. *Soviet Policy for the 1980s*. Bloomington, In.: Indiana University Press, 1983.

Brzezinski, Zbigniew. *The Grand Failure: The Birth and Death of Communism in the Twentieth Century*. New York: Scribners, 1989.

Cameron, Ross. *Local Government in the Soviet Union: Problems of Implementation and Control*. New York: St. Martin's, 1987.

Cimbala, Stephen, and John Starron, Jr., eds. *The Soviet Challenge in the Nineteen Nineties*. New York: Praeger, 1989.

Clemens, Walter C., Jr. *Can Russia Change: The U.S.S.R. Confronts Global Interdependence*. Boston, Ma.: Unwin Hyman, 1989.

Cohen, Stephen F. *Sovieticus: American Perceptions and Soviet Reality*. New York: W. W. Norton, 1986.

Collins, Joseph J. *The Soviet Invasion of Afghanistan: A Study in the Use of Force in Soviet Foreign Policy*. Lexington, Ma.: Lexington Books, 1988.

Colton, Timothy J. *The Dilemma of Reform in the Soviet Union*, revised and enlarged ed. New York: Council on Foreign Relations, 1986.

Conquest, Robert. *Power and Policy in the U.S.S.R.: The Struggle for Stalin's Succession, 1945–1960*. New York: Harper, 1967.

Conte, Francis, and Jean-Louis Matres, eds. *The Soviet Union in International Relations*. New York: St. Martin's, 1987.

Deibel, Terry L., and John Lewis Gaddis, eds. *Containing the Soviet Union*. Elmsford, N.Y.: Pergamon-Brassey's, 1987.

Desai, Padma. *Perestroika in Perspective: The Design and Dilemmas of Soviet Reform*. Princeton, N.J.: Princeton University Press, 1989.

Dibb, Paul. *The Soviet Union: The Incomplete Superpower*. Champaign, Ill.: University of Illinois Press, 1986.

Doder, Dusko. *Shadows and Whispers: Power Politics inside the Kremlin from Brezhnev to Gorbachev*. New York: Penguin, 1988.

Donnelly, Christopher, ed. *Gorbachev's Revolution: Economic Pressures and Defense Realities*. Alexandria, Va.: Janes Information, 1989.

English, Robert O., and Jonathan J. Halpern. *The Other Side: How Soviets and Americans Perceive Each Other*. New Brunswick, N.J.: Transaction, 1987.

Fulbright, J. W. *Old Myths and New Realities*. New York: Random House, 1964.

Fulbright, J. W., with Seth P. Tillman. *The Price of Empire*. New York: Pantheon, 1989.

Gaddis, John L. *Russia, the Soviet Union and the United States: An Interpretive History*, 2d ed. New York: McGraw-Hill, 1989.

Garthoff, Raymond. *Détente and Confrontation*. Washington, D.C.: Brookings, 1985.

Gelman, Harry. *The Brezhnev Politburo and the Decline of Détente*. Ithaca, N.Y.: Cornell University Press, 1984.

George, Alexander L., Philip J. Farley, and Alexander Dallin, eds. *U.S.–Soviet Security Cooperation: Achievements, Failures, Lessons*. New York: Oxford University Press, 1988.

George, Alexander L., ed. *Managing U.S. Soviet Rivalry: Problems of Crisis Prevention*. Boulder, Co.: Westview, 1983.

Gerner, Kristian, and Stefan Hedlund. *Ideology and Rationality in the Soviet Model: A Legacy for Gorbachev*. New York: Routledge, Chapman and Hall, 1989.

Gleason, Gregory. *National Federalism in the U.S.S.R.* Boulder, Co.: Westview, 1988.

Golan, Galia. *The Soviet Union and National Liberation Movements in the Third World*. Boston, Ma.: Unwin Hyman, 1988.

Gong, Gerrit W., Angela E. Stent, and Rebecca V. Strode, *Areas of Challenge for Soviet Foreign Policy in the 1980s*. Bloomington, In.: Indiana University Press, 1985.

Goodpaster, Andrew J., Walter J. Stoessel, Jr., and Robert Kennedy, eds. *U.S. Policy toward the Soviet Union: A Long Term Perspective 1987– 2000*. Lanham, Md.: University Press of America, 1988.

Gorbachev, Mikhail. *Perestroika—New Thinking for Our Country and the World*. New York: Harper and Row, 1987.

Gromyko, Anatoly, and Martin Hellman, eds. *Breakthrough: Emerging New Thinking*. New York: Walker and Company, 1988.

Hahn, Jeffery W. *Soviet Grassroots: Citizen Participation in Local Soviet Government*. Princeton, N.J.: Princeton University Press, 1988.

Hajda, Lubomyr, and Mark Beissinger, eds. *The Nationalities Factor in Soviet Society and Politics*. Boulder, Co.: Westview, 1989.

Harasymiw, Bohdan. *Political Elite Recruitment in the U.S.S.R.* New York: St. Martin's, 1984.

Hazan, Baruch. *From Brezhnev to Gorbachev: Infighting in the Kremlin*. Boulder, Co.: Westview, 1987.

Hazan, Baruch. *Gorbachev's Gamble: The Nineteenth All-Union Party Conference*. Boulder, Co.: Westview, 1989.

Herman, Paul F., Jr. *Thinking about Peace: The Conceptualization and Conduct of U.S.-Soviet Détente.* Lanham, Md.: University Press of America, 1987.

Hermann, Richard K. *Perceptions and Behavior in Soviet Foreign Policy.* Pittsburgh, Pa.: University of Pittsburgh Press, 1985.

Hewett, Ed A. *Energy, Economics and Foreign Policy in the Soviet Union. Washington, D.C.: Brookings, 1984.*

————. *Reforming the Soviet Economy: Equality versus Efficiency.* Washington, D.C.: Brookings, 1988.

Hirsch, Steve. *Memo: New Soviet Voices on Foreign and Economic Poicy.* Washington, D.C.: BNA Books, 1989.

Hohmann, Hans-Hermann, Alec Nove, and Heinrich Vogel. *Economics and Politics in the U.S.S.R.: Problems of Interdependence.* Boulder, Co.: Westview, 1986.

Horelick, Arnold L., ed. *U.S.-Soviet Relations: The Next Phase.* Ithaca, N.Y.: Cornell University Press, 1986.

Hough, Jerry F. *Opening up the Soviet Economy.* Washington, D.C.: Brookings, 1988.

————. *Russia and the West: Gorbachev and the Politics of Reform.* New York: Simon and Schuster, 1988.

Huber, Robert T. *Soviet Perceptions of the U.S. Congress: The Impact on Superpower Relations.* Boulder, Co.: Westview, 1988.

Jamgotch, Nish, Jr., ed. *Sectors of Mutual Benefit in U.S.–Soviet Relations.* Durham, N.C.: Duke University Press, 1985.

————. *U.S.–Soviet Cooperation: A New Future.* New York: Praeger, 1989.

Jonsson, Christer. *Superpower: Comparing American and Soviet Foreign Policy.* New York: St. Martin's, 1984.

Kanet, Roger E., ed. *Soviet Foreign Policy and East-West Relations.* Elmsford, N.Y.: Pergamon, 1982.

Keeble, Curtis, ed. *The Soviet State: The Domestic Roots of Soviet Foreign Policy.* Boulder, Co.: Westview, 1984.

Kelley, Donald R. *Soviet Policy from Brezhnev to Gorbachev.* New York: Praeger, 1988.

Killen, Linda R. *The Soviet Union and the U.S.: A New Look at the Cold War.* Boston, Ma: G. K. Hall, 1988.

Kintner, William R. *Soviet Global Strategy.* Fairfax, Va.: Hero Books, 1988.

Klugman, Jeffery. *The New Soviet Elite: How They Think and What They Want.* New York: Praeger, 1989.

Kolkowicz, Roman, ed. *The Roots of Soviet Power: Domestic Determinants of Foreign and Defense Policy.* Boulder, Co.: Westview, 1988.

Kolodziej, Edward A., and Roger E. Kanet, eds. *The Limits of Soviet Power in the Developing World.* Baltimore, Md.: Johns Hopkins University Press, 1989.

Krickus, R. J. *The Superpowers in Crisis: Implications of Domestic Discord.* Elmsford, N.Y.: Pergamon, 1987.

Laird, Robbin F., and Erik P. Hoffman, eds. *Soviet Foreign Policy in a Changing World.* Hawthorne, N.Y.: Aldine de Gruyter, 1986.

Lane, David. *State and Politics in U.S.S.R.* New York: New York University Press, 1985.

—. *Elites and Political Power in the U.S.S.R.* Brookfield, Vt.: Gower, 1988.

Lenczowski, John. *Soviet Perceptions of U.S. Foreign Policy.* Ithaca, N.Y.: Cornell University Press, 1982.

Light, Margot. *The Soviet Theory of International Relations.* New York: St. Martin's, 1988.

Linden, Carl A. *The Soviet Party–State: Aspects of Ideocratic Despotism.* New York: Praeger, 1983.

Liska, George. *Russia and the Road to Appeasement: Cycles of East–West Conflict in War and Peace.* Baltimore, Md.: Johns Hopkins University Press, 1982.

Lynch, Allen. *The Soviet Study of International Relations.* New York: Cambridge University Press, 1987.

—. *Gorbachev's International Outlook: Intellectual Origins and Political Consequences.* Boulder, Co.: Westview, 1989.

Maddock, R. T. *The Political Economy of Soviet Defense Spending.* New York: St. Martin's, 1988.

MccGwire, Michael. *Military Objectives in Soviet Foreign Policy.* Washington, D.C.: Brookings, 1987.

—. *Perestroika and Soviet National Security.* Washington, D.C.: Brookings, 1988.

Mellville, Andrei. *How We View Each Other: The Enemy Image and New Political Thinking.* Moscow: Novosti Press Agency Publishing House, 1988.

Mellville, Andrei, and Gail W. Lapidus, eds. *The Glasnost Papers: Voices on Reform from Moscow.* Boulder, Co.: Westview, 1989.

Menon, Rajan, and Daniel N. Nelson. *Limits to Soviet Power.* Lexington, Ma.: Lexington Books, 1989.

Miller, James R., ed. *Politics, Work and Daily Life in the U.S.S.R.: A Survey of Former Soviet Citizens.* New York: Cambridge University Press, 1987.

Miller, William G., ed. *Toward a More Civil Society: U.S.–Soviet Relations.* New York: Ballinger, 1989.

Mlynar, Zdenek. *Can Gorbachev Change the Soviet Union? The International Dimension of Political Reform.* Boulder, Co.: Westview, 1989.

Naylor, Thomas H. *The Gorbachev Strategy: Opening the Closed Society*. Lexington, Ma.: Lexington Books, 1987.

Nelson, Daniel N., and Roger B. Anderson, eds. *Soviet–American Relations: Understanding Differences, Avoiding Conflicts*. Wilmington, De.: Scholarly Resources Inc., 1988.

Nerlich, Uwe, ed. *Soviet Power and Western Negotiating Policies*. Vol. 2, *The Western Panacea; Constraining Soviet Power through Negotiating*. New York: Ballinger, 1983.

Nicic, Miroslav. *Anatomy of Hostility: The U.S.–Soviet Rivalry in Perspective*. New York: Harcourt Brace Jovanovich, 1989.

Nogee, Joseph L., and Robert Donaldson. *Soviet Foreign Policy since World War II*. 3d ed. Elmsford, N.Y.: Pergamon, 1988.

Nogee, Joseph L., and John W. Spainer. *Peace Impossible—War Unlikely: The Cold War between the United States and the Soviet Union*. Glenview, Il.: Scott, Foresman, 1988.

Papp, Daniel S. *Soviet Perceptions of the Developing World During the 1980s: The Ideological Basis*. Lexington, Ma.: Lexington Books, 1985.

Payne, Richard J. *Opportunities and Dangers of Soviet–Cuban Expansion: Toward a Pragmatic U.S. Policy*. Albany, N.Y.: State University of New York Press, 1988.

Potichnyj, Peter J., ed. *Soviet Union: Party and Society*. New York: Cambridge University Press, 1988.

Pravda, Alex. *Soviet Foreign Policy: Priorities under Gorbachev*. New York: Routledge, Chapman & Hall, 1988.

Pushkarev, Sergie. *Self-Government and Freedom in Russia*. Boulder, Co.: Westview, 1988.

Ramet, Pedro, ed. *Religion and Nationalism in Soviet and East European Politics*. Durham, N.C.: Duke University Press, 1988.

Remington, Thomas F. *The Truth of Authority: Ideology and Communication in the Soviet Union*. Pittsburgh, Pa.: University of Pittsburgh Press, 1989.

Rose, Clive. *The Soviet Propaganda Network: A Directory of Organizations Serving Soviet Foreign Policy*. New York: St. Martin's, 1989.

Rourke, John T. *Making Foreign Policy—United States, Soviet Union and China*. Pacific Grove, Ca.: Brooks/Cole, 1990.

Rubinstein, Alvin Z. *Soviet Foreign Policy since World War II: Imperial and Global*. 3d ed. Glenview, Ill.: Scott, Foresman, 1989.

Ryavec, Karl W. *United States–Soviet Relations*. New York: Longman, 1988.

Saiveta, Carol R., and Sylvia Edgington. *Soviet–Third World Relations*. Boulder, Co.: Westview, 1985.

Sakharov, Andrei D. *Sakharov Speaks*. New York: Alfred A. Knopf, 1974.

Savigear, Peter. *Cold War or Detente in the Nineteen Eighties: The International Politics of American–Soviet Relations*. New York: St. Martin's, 1987.

Sherr, Alan B. *The Other Side of Arms Control: Soviet Objectives in the Gorbachev Era*. Boston, Ma.: Unwin Hyman, 1988.

Shlapentokh, Vladimir. *Sociology and Politics: The Soviet Case*. Falls Church, Va.: Delphic, 1985.

Shlapentokh, Vladimir, and Dmitry Shlapentokh. *Soviet Ideologies in the Period of Glasnost: Responses to Brezhnev's Stagnation*. New York: Praeger, 1988.

Smith, Gordon B. *Soviet Politics—Continuity and Contradiction*. New York: St. Martin's, 1988.

Snow, Donald M., ed. *Soviet-American Security Relations in the 1990s*. Lexington, Ma.: Lexington Books, 1989.

Sonnenfeld, Helmut. *Soviet Politics in the Nineteen Eighties*. Boulder, Co.: Westview, 1984.

Staar, Richard F. *U.S.S.R. Foreign Policies after Détente*. rev. ed. Stanford, Ca.: Hoover Institution, 1987.

Stein, Johnathan B. *The Soviet Bloc, Energy and Western Security*. Lexington, Ma.: Lexington Books, 1983.

Stevenson, Richard W. *The Rise and Fall of Détente: Relaxations of Tension in U.S.–Soviet Relations 1953–1984*. Champaign, Ill.: University of Illinois Press, 1985.

Trofimenko, Henry, and Pavel Podlesny. *USSR–USA Lessons of Peaceful Coexistence*. Moscow: Novosti Press Agency Publishing House, 1988.

Valenta, Jiri, and W. C. Potter, eds. *Soviet Decision Making for National Security*. Boston, Ma.: Unwin Hyman, 1984.

Veen, Hans-Joachim, ed. *From Brezhnev to Gorbachev: Domestic Affairs & Soviet Foreign Policy*. New York: St. Martin's, 1987.

Vigor, V. H. *The Soviet View of Disarmament*. New York: St. Martin's, 1986.

Von Beyme, Klaus. *The Soviet Union and International Policies*. New York: St. Martin's, 1987.

Walker, Martin. *The Waking Giant: Gorbachev's Russia*. New York: Patheon, 1986.

———. *Martin Walker's Russia*. London: Michael Joseph, 1989.

Weihmiller, Gordon R., and Dusko Doder. *U.S.–Soviet Summits: An Account of East–West Diplomacy at the Top 1955–1985*. Lanham, Md.: University Press of America, 1986.

Wells, Samuel F., and Robert S. Litwak, eds. *Strategic Defenses and Soviet–American Relations*. New York: Ballinger, 1987.

Wettig, Gerhard. *High Road, Low Road: Diplomacy and Public Action in Soviet Foreign Policy*. Elmsford, N.Y.: Pergamon, 1989.

White, Ralph F. *Fearful Warriors: A Psychological Profile of U.S.–Soviet Relations*. New York: Free Press, 1989.

White, Stephen, and Alex Pravda, eds. *Ideology and Soviet Politics*. New York: St. Martin's, 1988.

Wimbush, Enders S., et al. *Glasnost and Empire: National Aspirations in the U.S.S.R.* Munich: Radio Free Europe, 1989.

Woodby, Sylvia. *Gorbachev and the Decline of Ideology in Soviet Foreign Policy*. Boulder, Co.: Westview, 1989.

Zemstoy, Ilya. *Lexicon of Soviet Political Terms*. Fairfax, Va.: Hero Books, 1985.

Index

About the Editors and Contributors

DONALD R. KELLEY is a senior research fellow at the Fulbright Institute, University of Arkansas, professor of political science, and director of the Russian and Soviet Studies Program. He is editor of the *Modern Encyclopedia of Russia and the Soviet Union*, a projected 50–volume work covering all aspects of twentieth century Russia and the Soviet Union. He has B.A. and M.A. degrees from the University of Pittsburgh, and a Ph.D. from Indiana University, and he was an exchange student at Moscow State University. His books include *Soviet Politics from Brezhnev to Gorbachev, The Politics of Developed Socialism: The Soviet Union as a Postindustrial State, The Solzhenitsyn–Sakharov Dialogue, Soviet Politics in the Brezhnev Era* (editor and contributor), and *The Economic Superpowers and the Environment*. He has also contributed to a number of journals and anthologies.

HOYT PURVIS is director of the Fulbright Institute at the University of Arkansas and teaches journalism and political science. He served as foreign/defense policy advisor to Senate Majority Leader Robert Byrd; deputy director, Senate Democratic Policy Committee; and press secretary-special assistant to Senator J. W. Fulbright. Among the issues he worked on were arms control and U.S.–Soviet relations.

He served as senior research fellow and taught at the Lyndon B. Johnson School of Public Affairs, University of Texas. He is author or editor of several books including *The Presidency and the Press* and *Legislating Foreign Policy*.

TIMOTHY J. COLTON is professor of government at Harvard University. He was formerly director of the Center for Russian and East European Studies at the University of Toronto. He has a Ph.D. from Harvard and B.A. and M.A. degrees from Toronto. He has been a fellow of the Kennan Institute for Advanced Russian Studies and a visiting professor and lecturer at a number of leading institutions. He has been codirector of projects on trends in civil–military relations in the Soviet Union and on Canadian–Soviet relations. His books include *Commissars, Commanders, and Civilian Authority: The Structure of Soviet Military Politics* and *The Dilemma of Reform in the Soviet Union*. He has contributed to a number of books and journals.

ROBERT K. GERMAN is a former career diplomat who has specialized in Soviet affairs and U.S.–Soviet relations and has been a visiting professor at the Lyndon B. Johnson School of Public Affairs, University of Texas. He served three tours of duty at the American Embassy in Moscow, most recently in 1979–80 when he was counselor for political affairs. In Washington he served as the State Department's Soviet Desk director and as director of the Office of Analysis of the School of Area Studies at the State Department's Foreign Service Institute. He is the editor of *The Future of U.S.– U.S.S.R. Relations: Lessons from Forty Years without World War*. He has B.A. and J.D. degrees from the University of Texas.

JERRY F. HOUGH is director of the Center on East–West Trade, Investment, and Communications, James B. Duke professor of political science and public policy studies at Duke University, and a senior fellow at the Brookings Institution. His many books include *Soviet Leadership in Transition, The Struggle for the Third World: Soviet Debates and American Options, Opening Up the Soviet Economy, Russia and the West*. He is a frequent commentator on national news and public affairs programs.

WILLIAM G. MILLER is president of the American Committee on U.S.–Soviet Relations and of the International Foundation for the Survival and Development of Humanity. He has held a number of important governmental positions. After serving as a foreign service officer in Iran, he was special assistant to Senator John Sherman Cooper for foreign affairs and defense; staff director of the Senate Special Committee on National Emergency Powers; staff director of the Senate Select Committee to Study Governmental Operations with Respect to Intelligence Activities (Church Committee); staff director of the Senate Select Committee on Intelligence; and presidential emissary to Iran. He was associate dean and adjunct professor of international politics at the Fletcher School of Law and Diplomacy, Tufts University. He has been a fellow of the Institute of Politics at Harvard University and a faculty associate of the Center for Middle Eastern Studies at Harvard. He was cochairman of the National Academy of Public Administration Project on U.S.–U.S.S.R. Communications.

JOSEPH L. NOGEE is a professor of political science at the University of Houston. He has degrees from Georgetown University, the University of Chicago, and a Ph.D. from Yale University. He is author, coauthor, or editor of a lengthy list of books, including *Soviet Foreign Policy since World War II*, *Soviet Politics: Russia after Brezhnev*, *Peace Impossible–War Unlikely*, *The Cold War in U.S.–Soviet Relations*, and *Congress, the Presidency, and American Foreign Policy*. He has served as chairman of the Department of Political Science and director of the Russian Studies Program at the University of Houston and has been a visiting professor at the University of Virginia.

VLADIMIR O. PECHATNOV is first secretary of the Soviet Embassy in Washington and the representative of the Institute of USA and Canadian Studies of the U.S.S.R. Academy of Sciences. He graduated from the Moscow Institute of International Relations in 1970 and has served with the Institute of USA and Canadian Studies since 1972, where he headed the section on U.S. political institutions. In 1974 he completed his dissertation on the Democratic Party. He was a visiting scholar at Columbia University in 1976–77. His publications include two books, *Hamilton and Jefferson* and *The Democratic Party in the United States* (both in Russian), and numerous articles on U.S. political history and institutions.

HAROLD D. PIPER is editor of the Op-Ed page of the *Baltimore Sun*. He is a graduate of Princeton University and the University of Maryland School of Law. He has held a number of staff positions on the *Sun* and served as foreign correspondent in Moscow (1975–79), Bonn (1980–83), and London (1983–86). He was a professional journalism fellow at Stanford University. He won citations from the Overseas Press Club of New York in 1978 for a series on the Soviet Union and in 1984 for a series on arms control.

KARL W. RYAVEC is a professor of political science at the University of Massachusetts, where he teaches courses on Soviet politics, U.S.–Soviet relations, and related subjects. He has a Ph.D. from Columbia University. He was a senior IREX exchange scholar in the Soviet Union and has been a fellow of the Russian Research Center at Harvard University. He has served as director of Soviet and East College Faculty Seminar on Soviet Studies. He is author of the recently published book *United States–Soviet Relations* and has written or contributed to several other books and published a number of articles.

RICHARD F. STAAR is coordinator of the International Studies Program at the Hoover Institution. He served as U.S. ambassador to the Mutual and Balanced Reduction of Forces Negotiations (1981–83) in Vienna. His areas of specialization include the Soviet Union, Eastern Europe, arms control, and public diplomacy. He is a graduate of Dickinson College (B.A.) and Yale University (M.A.), and he has been a professor at Emory University and visiting professor at the Naval War College and National War College. His books include *USSR Foreign Policies after Détente* and *Communist Regimes in Eastern Europe*. He has contributed to a number of books and journals and serves on several editorial boards. He has been a consultant to the Defense Department and Arms Control and Disarmament Agency.

ENNO VON LOEWENSTERN is editorial page editor and deputy chief editor of the influential German newspaper *Die Welt*, and he is based in Bonn. He has been with *Die Welt* since 1972 and a journalist for 40 years. He is a well-known commentator on politics and public affairs and specializes on Eastern Europe and on legal/constitutional questions in Germany. He is also a contributing columnist for the *Wall Street Journal*.

MARTIN WALKER is U.S. correspondent for *The Guardian* (London and Manchester), based in Washington, D.C. He was a Brackenbury scholar at Balliol College, Oxford University, with first class honors in modern history; a Harkness fellow at Harvard University; and an American Political Science Association Congressional fellow. He was reporter of the year in Great Britain in 1987. He has published a number of fiction and non-fiction books. His non-fiction books include *Powers of the Press*, a comparative study of the world's leading newspapers; *The Waking Giant: Gorbachev's Russia*; *Martin Walker's Russia*; and *The Independent Traveler's Guide to the Soviet Union*.